On Final Approach

Author & Publisher
Edward C. Carr
Coupeville, Washington 98239

Typesetting & Layout
Whidbey Printers
1330 SW Barlow Street Suite 1
Oak Harbor, Washington 98277

ISBN 0-9721178-0-6

Second through Thirteenth Printing (in 2012)
by Gorham Printing
Centralia, Washington, USA

Ed Carr

Dedication

To The Crew

Acknowledgements

Gathering information for this history required help from the air crew members. The photos, documents, war diaries; but most particularly the stories and memories they shared, were appreciated beyond measure.

The histories of the 381ˢᵗ Bomb Group by Dave Osborne and Chaplain Brown enabled me to cross–check facts. One fact reported by Chaplain Brown set me on a frustrating search. That fact was that on June 9, 1945 Gene Nelson, our navigator, was awarded the Distinguished Flying Cross. Gene left England before June and never received the citation or the medal. I wanted to track it down and include the DFC citation in this book. I regret that neither the Air Force Research Agency, Maxwell AFB or the National Personnel record Center in St. Louis could locate the citation. The Records center had a fire in 1973 that destroyed many records. I thank both agencies for their efforts.

The 381ˢᵗ Bomb Group web site was helpful and led me to a great source of detailed information on the January 10, 1945 mission. The research librarians and museum volunteers that I contacted came up with some amazing information on World War II Army Air Bases.

To complete this project I needed a skilled typist—someone who could read my writing, correct my spelling, proof read the manuscript and give advice on both sentence structure and English usage. I needed a master language arts teacher with exceptional office skills just like Jan, my wife, who did all of the above and much more.

Ed Carr
Coupeville, Washington
2002

Under Acknowledgements on the preceding page, it is stated that Gene Nelson, our navigator, was awarded the Distinguished Flying Cross on 9 June 1945, but never received it. After 58 years he was finally presented with the DFC by US Congressman Thomas Petri at a ceremony in Fond du Lac, Wisconsin on 27 August 2003.

Table of Contents

INTRODUCTION

This is a collection of stories about an aircrew of a B-17 Flying Fortress during World War II. In starting this writing, my aim was to record and portray the events of that time as a history of our crew, written for our air crew. Others may find this an interesting historical record of the air war from the perspective of one bomber crew—history from the ground up.

To preserve the record of the men in our air crew may have been my original motive, but it turned out to be not the only motive for this writing. With the passage of time it becomes more difficult to believe what we really did in those war years of 1944 and 1945. That it was nine young men with minimal training, flying a heavy bomber across the North Atlantic and then on missions over Germany. The Army Air Force designated the pilot as the airplane commander of a B-17. Probably then, it is my responsibility to preserve these stories, our stories, and by recording them make them real again and confirm that we were part of such an extraordinary group of men, an air crew.

But is there any need, or a valid reason, for another remembrance or memoir of the war years? Is there any purpose to the efforts of a retiree to piece together the stories of those exciting younger years? Are there gaps in the history of the period, still untold stories? As of the summer of 2000, veterans of World War II are reportedly dying at the rate of 1,000 per day. Still with reliable memory, those of us lucky to be alive and healthy should tell their stories if only to provide a primary source for future historians. The Mighty Eighth Air Force Heritage Museum has requested information on aircrew experiences for their archives. That may be sufficient reason for this writing. The grandchildren or great grandchildren of crew members may someday pull these pages from a trunk and better understand the part grandfather played in the big war. Hopefully these pages may help explain who we were and what we did

For them, Gene Nelson, Ellis Richard, Rudy Staszko, Hugh Treadwell, and those no longer with us, Dave Phillips, Al Hines, and Bob Whitaker; and Bill Collins, who reportedly returned to England, I am writing this history. It is a shared history from 14 April 1944, when we were activated as an air crew for training, to our flight to Britain in July, to 5 August 1944 when we reported to the 381st Bomb Group and through the fall of 1944 and early 1945 when we flew from our base in England.

To provide background on the crew I will go back to earlier days, who we were and where we came from. Our later days with the Bomb Group in England will be covered in some detail to explain how our survival from the perils and dangers of the air war, from our own blunders and some command blunders, has given us a bond and a common memory of events that has endured over many years.

On 8 July 1944 we were given secret orders for our flight to Britain. Those orders stipulated that we could not send safe arrival telegrams from the stops on our flight across the Atlantic. We were allowed to write letters. I still have the letter I wrote home on 12 July 1944 from "Somewhere in Iceland." In the letter is this rather tentative understatement: "Still have the same crew that I started with in Dyersburg and they have turned out swell. Hope they don't break us up because I would not want to lose any of them." Four days earlier, as a green B-17 air crew, we had left Nebraska on the first leg of our flight across the Atlantic to Britain; then on to our Eighth Air Force base in England, at Ridgewell in Essex.

We had trained together for a couple of months, but we were now on our own. I knew then and I know now how lucky I was to have drawn this crew. The trust and friendship between flyers in an air crew are difficult to explain. I will try.

The history of the 20th Century is anchored in the war years, 1940 through 1945. In those years the major symbol of the military air power and the industrial might of America was the B-17 Flying Fortress. It was our first weapon to strike at Hitler's homeland. Also it was the most easily recognized aircraft of World War II. Although the B-24 Liberator played a big part in the European air war, the Fort, or the Big-Assed Bird, as it was affectionately known, was the first and primary heavy bomber used by the airmen of the Eighth Air Force. An axiom of aircraft design is that an aircraft flies like it looks. The B-24 looked like a truck. Pilots didn't fly a B-24; they drove it. The B-17 had graceful design lines. When under a proper trim, it flew itself. A very forgiving airplane, it was also probably one of the most rugged ever built. We who flew in the Fortress knew that, in part, our chance of survival was enhanced by our plane. Against all odds, the B-17 got crews back to England when other aircraft with similar damage would have gone down. Our crew, as others, became emotionally attached to the 17.

Many books have been written, movies produced and television programs made telling the stories of bomber crews of the Eighth Air Force flying from England during the war. I have listed titles in the bibliography. They have explained the grand strategies of the major air battles and the part played by the airmen in the defeat of Germany.

That the Eighth Air Force had the highest casualty rate of all United States military units in World War II attests to the violence and danger that crews faced in the air war over Germany. Most crew members, however, will agree that their first great adventure was not from an airbase in England. The initial challenge for a rookie crew was getting there, flying their new bomber across the Atlantic Ocean to Britain.

Most all heavy bombers, B-17's and B-24's, destined for the 8th Air Force in England or the 15th Air Force in Italy were flown by new crews across the North Atlantic or by the southerly route via South America and North Africa. To get to the United Kingdom (the UK) most B-17 crews like ours leap frogged across the North Atlantic using airfields built for that purpose. The names of these fields were legendary: "Goose" in Labrador, "Gander" in Newfoundland, "Meeks" in Iceland, and the emergency air strips in Greenland—"BW One" and "BW Two." The Air Transport Command (ATC) planes routinely flew the route, but it wasn't routine for a new bomber crew. The flight across was an air crew's first long trip which was not under the control of the Training Command. On our own for the first time, the initial take-off almost had the same feeling as a first solo flight in Primary Training. The crew still had doubts about our separate roles. Could we rely on each other? With no experience flying over water there was obvious apprehension about the ocean crossing ahead. But there was still an eagerness to get going—over there—to what we didn't know. What to expect was learned from war stories told by our instructors, many of whom were veterans of the air war in Europe.

Before the flight, the crew had just finished what was known as Phase Training, a period of a little more than two months when newly formed crews were readied for combat. The pilot was the airplane commander and in charge of the crew. He would have spent ninety days in Transition School learning to fly the B-17 before reporting to Phase Training School. Total time logged in the Flying Fortress was about 100 hours. Typically the copilot reported to Phase Training just after graduating from Advanced Flight Training in a twin-engine trainer like the Cessna AT-17. That light trainer was jokingly referred to as the Bamboo Bomber or the Double Breasted Cub. Most copilots had never been in a B-17. None of the other crew members, except for the flight engineer, were familiar with the multi engine Flying Fortress. After a little more than two months in Phase School crew training, the Army Air Force would hand over a brand new B-17 G and tell us to fly it to England.

In 35 (or more) missions flown with the 381st Bomb Group from Ridgewell, Essex, England, our crew experienced the air combat over Europe described in the many books and films. While some of those experiences will be described, this is also the story of our start as a crew, our big adventure or misadventure of getting there in a new, fresh-off-the-assembly line Boeing B-17 Flying Fortress.

After completing Phase Training in Dyersburg, Tennessee, we were sent by train to Kearney, Nebraska. We took off from Kearney AAF in our new B-17 heading for Britain. The flight across was made in four legs:

One—Kearney AAF Nebraska to Grenier AAF.
Manchester, New Hampshire

Two—Grenier AAF to Goose AAF at
Goose Bay, Labrador

Three—Goose AAF to Meeks AAF at
Keflavik, Iceland

Four—Meeks AAF to Valley, Wales, an airbase
under British command.

From Valley, Wales, we traveled by rail to Stone, England. Near Stoke on Trent, Stone was the location of the 14th and 16th Replacement Depots. From Stone the enlisted crew went on to the 1st Combat Crew Gunnery School, Station 172, at Snettisham, near the "Wash" in East Anglia. The officers went to the 11th Combat Crew Replacement Center, Station 112, at Bovingdon, NW of London. After a few weeks the crew reassembled at our assigned Bomb Group, the 381st at Ridgewell, Essex, England.

Consultations with the crew members have helped reconcile memory differences of events. New anecdotes are frequently mentioned in telephone conversations, correspondence with the crew and at reunions. I have received photographs of our time together that I had never seen before. Gene Nelson gave me a copy of the mini diary he kept during the war years. It was very helpful. We have had the opportunity to rehash our experiences at five meetings since 1945. In 1978 Rudy Staszko and his wife Marg hosted a reunion in Omaha of five crew members. In 1985 seven met at our home in Kirkland, Washington. In 1995 four crew members, encouraged by Ellis Richard, gathered at a San Francisco reunion of the 381st Bomb Group. In September of 2000 three of us, Ellis, Gene and I met for a three day reunion at Gene's place in Neshkoro, Wisconsin. Ellis Richard, Hugh Treadwell, and Gene Nelson got together at our Whidbey Island home in 2001. Army Air Force records and documents have helped pin down and clarify events. I realize that anecdotal stories tend, over the years, to become more dramatic in the retelling. In collecting these stories I find that the facts need no elaboration. Any errors in recollection and in the telling of our story are mine. I do admit to a bias in describing members of our air crew.

PROLOGUE

Prologue—a preliminary course of action foreshadowing greater events. The story of our air crew as a unit begins with Chapter 1, when we first met to train together for combat. But we had to go through preparatory schooling before then. Early in the war years the Army Air Force developed plans to train and ready flyers for combat. Special skills would be needed on bomber crews. Before assembling for combat crew training, each member had to be proficient at his job. When we met at Dyersburg AAF for combat training each of us had undergone special schooling to qualify for a position on a B-17.

Our gunners Bob Whitaker (tail), Bill Collins (waist), Dave Phillips (ball turret) had completed aerial gunnery school. Their training included learning skills firing the 50-caliber machine gun, maintaining the weapon and operating gun turrets. Al Hines (radio operator) and Rudy Staszko (flight engineer) had also qualified at gunnery school. Radio technical school for Al demanded proficiency in the use of radio equipment, knowledge of radio communication systems, and the use of Morse code. Flight engineers like Rudy went through aircraft engine schools and learned about electrical and hydraulic aircraft systems.

After preflight school, bombardiers were trained in the use of the Norden bombsight, bomb ordinance and bomb shackling systems. Because the Norden bombsight was one of our most closely guarded secrets, a bombardier had to take an oath to protect it with his life. The special oath read, "Mindful of the secret trust about to be placed in me by the Commander in Chief, the President of the United States, by whose direction I have been chosen for bombardier training—and mindful of the fact that I am to become guardian of one of my country's most priceless military assets, the American bombsight—I do here, in the presence of Almighty God, swear by the Bombardier's Code of Honor to keep inviolate the secrecy of any and all confidential information revealed to me, and further to uphold the honor and integrity of the Army Air Forces, if need be, with my life itself." At bombardier school, records were kept of practice bomb hits and misses. The elimination rate for cadets was about 12%. Hugh Treadwell would have dropped about 160 practice bombs. Bombardiers got some navigation training and went to gunnery school as well.

It really helped if a navigator cadet had a background in mathematics or engineering. Navigators were trained in precision dead reckoning, pilotage, and radio and celestial navigation. They would have spent approximately 100 hours in the air and five hours in the classroom for every one in the air. Gene Nelson, our navigator, has told me of the tough final flight test that he had to pass to qualify. Navigators also completed aerial gunnery school.

I do not have first hand knowledge of what these schools were like. My experience before reporting to Dyersburg for combat crew training was in pilot training, learning to fly a small trainer and then gradually moving up to a heavy bomber, the B-17. To get their wings all pilots, after pre-flight school, went through primary, basic and advanced flight schools. I went through flight schools in the West Coast Training Command. Ellis Richard, our copilot, took all of his flight training in west Texas flight schools. The training requirements would have been the same in both places. Graduating from advanced school a pilot received either an assignment to a combat crew as a copilot of a multi-engine plane or was sent to transition flight school to learn to fly combat air craft or transport planes. Those of us sent to B-17 transition school were expected to become first pilots and crew commanders, although some in mid 1944 went on to B-29 flight school.

The following pages will describe the schools and training that enabled me to arrive at Dyersburg in April 1944 as a qualified B-17 pilot. The description of my pilot training is not unique. While this is my personal story, it could probably apply as typical for the majority of World War II Army Air Force pilots.

Pre Flight

Before starting our actual flight training, the Army Air Force required attendance at Pre Flight School. For cadets the Pre Flight School was similar to OCS (Officers Candidate School) of the other branches. They took typical military training, including a lot of drilling and physical training. The selection process continued with tests and screening to determine fitness for pilot, bombardier, or navigator school. It seemed that the cadets at Santa Ana Pre Flight were constantly in formation, double-timing it to class or other places on the base as they shouted cadence or sang to the rhythm of their march. Hazing by the upper class of the lower class was not uncommon.

Into this setting arrived the Student Officers. Because of the urgent need for flight officers the Army transferred, in grade, commissioned officers to the Air Force from other branches, hence the title Student Officer. In April 1943 I reported to Santa Ana Pre Flight School, Santa Ana, California, where I met up again with my Coast Artillery cohort, Lt. Ted Gilbert. Ted had facilitated our transfer to the Air Force, but more about his shenanigans later in this story. Assigned to the Flight School class of 43k we found out that compared to the cadets, the student officers would have much abbreviated orientation schooling at Pre Flight before going on to Primary Flight Schools. It probably should have been apparent to us that the Training Command was not too hot on the idea of student officers going through flight school along side of cadets. Maybe it was thought we would have a bad influence on our classmates.

Shortly after our arrival we were called to a meeting at the Base Theater for what we thought would be a briefing session and a welcome to the Army Air Force. The Commandant of the Pre Flight School addressed the assembled student officers. He emphasized how tough our flight training would be, that many of us would wash out. The rate of cadet washouts was about 40% and I assumed that applied to student officers. The Commandant stressed that we would be shown no favoritism and then made the ill-advised statement that, "It should be understood that we had earned our commissions the easy way!" The man obviously didn't know his audience. While Ted and I were OCS graduates, there were also in the audience of student officers some West Pointers, some lieutenants who had received battlefield commissions while engaged in jungle warfare and some others who had returned from combat duty in the Pacific. Some grumbling swept across the assembly and a few of the members started rising to their feet. Sensing that he had put his foot in his mouth, the speaker back tracked with an apology and was able to prevent a potential walkout. What a welcome to the Army Air Force!

I have little recollection of any class work at Santa Ana. We were given complete physical examinations and were required to be interviewed by an Army Air Force psychiatrist. The interview was to help determine our fitness for pilot training. The hard-nosed bunch of student officers thought the questioning was a joke. In a serious voice they would quote the good doctor: "Tell me your feelings. Do you like your sister more than your brother?"

It was evident that the Training Command wanted the student officers out of Pre Flight as soon as our processing was completed and we were gone in about three weeks. In the rush they forgot to schedule us for the required time in the altitude chamber. We had to return nine months later to fulfill that requirement.

Primary

After getting past some initial anxiety about flying, I found primary flight school an enjoyable experience. Student officers had been pushed through preflight school at Santa Ana, California, in about two weeks. Aviation cadets were there about two months. As part of the class 43-K I was assigned to Eagle Field in the San Joaquin Valley near Dos Palos, California. There was both an upper and lower class at Primary. The lower or following class to mine was designated 44-A. Student officers lived in off-base apartments within walking distance of the field. We went through ground school with the cadets. Subjects in ground school classes included The Theory of Flight, Air Craft Engines, Basic Navigation, Aircraft and Naval Ship Identification, Radio Communication and Weather. We were tested and graded in each class.

Our civilian flight instructors had a lot of experience in small planes. My instructor, F. A. Allen, was a great teacher and a terrific pilot. He had unlimited patience with my bonehead maneuvers and didn't push too fast. One's first solo flight was a big deal, but Allen played it down until he felt a student was ready. I had about 13 hours in the trainer before I soloed. The open cockpit, low wing Ryan PT-22 was a joy to fly. Its cruising speed was about 100 mph and its maximum speed 125 mph. A 160 horsepower

Kinner engine provided the power. The plane had a wingspan of 30 feet 1 inch and a weight of 1,860 lbs. maximum. It was a simple airplane; no radio, no intercom. Communication between student and instructor was by use of the gosport, a flexible tube connected to the earpiece of a flyer's helmet, with a mouthpiece at the other end. The instructor in the front seat would also use hand signals, but it would be the voice commands that students would remember best. "Keep your head on a swivel." "You've got it up and locked again." "Don't try to stretch your glide." "You're over controlling." "Keep the nose on the horizon."

After we soloed it was great fun to go skylarking over the valley in clear spring weather practicing spins, loops, rolls, etc. The only thing unpredictable about the PT-22 was the engine. It would conk out on occasion. Because of this we practiced forced landings almost touching down with power cut back, then pulling up. Over the valley farmland the main rule for a forced landing was to line up with the plowed furrows. We always kept watch for downed planes and reported them as soon as possible. I remember flying over a PT-22 sitting in a field with the student pilot waving as I flew over. It was Lt. Henthorn, a fellow student officer.

For a student officer life in Primary School was a positive experience. We were not hazed by the upper class cadets. Our main gripe was that we had to serve as "Officer of the Day" on weekends. I suspected that the Commandant of Cadets, a Captain, disliked student officers on principle. Perhaps I was wrong, but he or one of the other administrative officers put the student officers on the roster to be "Officers of the Day." Because we could not serve on that duty while on a flight training schedule, we were always given the assignment on weekends, which meant we did not get weekend leave. The Commandant and his fellow administrative officers always disappeared on weekends. The practice stopped when a high-ranking student officer came on base with the next lower class.

A nice woman from Dos Palos was manager of the student officers' apartments. She appointed herself "House Mother" to the student officers and arranged several weekend trips before we finished training at Primary. We went to Carmel and to San Francisco. She got all of us tickets to the operetta "The Firefly" at the Geary Theatre.

At Dos Palos I logged 65:10 hours in the PT-22. After passing the check ride with the Army Air Force Check Pilot, my civilian instructor took me up for a joy ride. He showed me some real acrobatics in the PT-22 and we flew up the San Joaquin River at tree top level.

One hundred ninety-four cadets and student officers graduated with the class of 43-K.

What a bunch of hot pilots we were! They took our graduation photo wearing a helmet, goggles pushed up and a white silk scarf. The class of 43-K put on a big graduation dance in the main hanger. Joe Reichman and his band came down from one of the San Francisco hotels to play for the dance. Girls were brought by bus from nearby towns for the party, which was mainly for the graduating cadets. We student officers hung around outside taking in the great band music.

The next day we headed south to our next duty station for Basic Flight School.

Basic

Basic Flight School was not the same as the joy ride we had in Primary. My Basic School was at Lemoore AAF near Hanford, California. It was now August, mid summer in the San Joaquin Valley and very hot. Now under military instructors we were to learn to fly the BT-15 Valiant, known throughout the training command as the Vultee Vibrator. A heavier plane at 4,227 lbs. with more instruments, radio equipment, a more powerful 450 HP Wright radial engine, an enclosed canopy over dual seats. It was the same plane as the BT-13 which had a Pratt and Whitney engine. This plane was a handful for a student to master. Just a few days after our arrival an upper class cadet had spun in a BT-15 killing himself.

A friend of mine and fellow student officer washed out at Lemoore. He told me that he was relieved because he never could feel in control of the plane. The day he washed out his instructor told him that the only thing he ever did right in the plane was the purely mechanical procedure for getting out of a spin—hit opposite rudder real hard and dump the stick. The problem was that most other maneuvers he tried ended in a spin.

I drew a strange flight instructor at Lemoore. I can't recall the lieutenant's name, but I don't think he was happy trying to teach us to fly the BT-15. He probably wanted to be flying a P-38. I was the only student officer in a flight of five students assigned to the lieutenant. The first day we reported to him on the flight line he looked us over, pointed to me and said, "As long as I have been teaching at this school one of my students has always been the first in the entire class to solo the BT-15 and since you are the ranking person in this flight, you are it!" I thought he was joking. Never having ever been in a BT-15, how could he judge my capability to handle the plane? True to his word, after only 4 $^1/_2$ hours under his instruction he announced one morning that I should get in a BT-15 and fly it to an auxiliary landing field where he would meet me with another student. I am sure that my mouth fell open, but I was not going to let him see my knees shaking so I grabbed a parachute and headed to the plane. Triple checking everything, I taxied to the end of the runway and requested clearance for take-off. I got off the ground ok; then it dawned on me that I wasn't sure of the location of the auxiliary landing strip. It was somewhere to the northwest according to my vague recollection. US Highway 99 was the main north-south arterial through the valley and just east of Lemoore. To the west was the north-south coastal range. So I figured out a pattern to search for the auxiliary field. Go west from Highway 99 toward the coastal range, then edge a little north in a turn back to the east; then a little north and turn west. I repeated this pattern back and forth across the valley until I spotted the field and saw my instructor on the ground madly waving his arms. It should have taken me only a few minutes for a direct flight to the auxiliary strip. I had been in the air much longer. After landing I taxied to where the lieutenant was waiting and cut the engine. He wanted to know where in the hell I had been. I told him that I was enjoying my first solo flight so much that I lost track of time. He accepted that as a reasonable explanation.

The Training Command decided to try an experiment when I was half way through Basic. The class would be split with some students completing basic training in the Advanced Trainer, the twin engine Cessna AT-17 Bobcat. With several other student officers I was put in this program. Our new instructor was an older officer, a captain, with a lot of experience. He was very relaxed and as a result a great teacher. He soon had us checked out in the AT-17, flying side by side with a fellow student. The fabric covered, wood and tubular steel AT-17 was powered by two 245 hp Jacobs radial engines. It could cruise at 150 mph but had a very low stalling speed. It weighed 5,700 lbs. with maximum load, but had a very low wing loading. It was commonly called the Bamboo Bomber or the Double Breasted Cub. In this plane we were introduced to instrument flying (under the hood), cross country and night flying.

I remember one night cross-country flight with a fellow student officer, an infantry 1st lieutenant, as my copilot. We were cruising at about 6,000 feet admiring the lights of the city of Fresno below us when both engines stopped. All of a sudden we were in a glide over the center of Fresno and thank God the AT-17 was a pretty good glider. The fuel gauges did not show we were on empty. We frantically tried to figure out what had happened as we descended over Fresno. The lieutenant said that he had switched fuel tanks by turning an overhead switch. I told him to try the switch again. He hadn't turned it all the way and in the mid position neither tank was feeding fuel to the engines. With the switch engaged, we started the engines, but we were down to about 1,000 feet. We had avoided a crash landing in the middle of Fresno! My friend was so completely unnerved by the experience he swore that the next morning he was going to hand in his resignation and return to the infantry. We talked him into staying and he went on to complete his flight training.

Because of the very low stalling speed the Cessna could be difficult to land in a strong cross wind. If a pilot took the plane out of its into-the-wind crab too soon before touch down, the side drift could wipe out the landing gear. We could slow fly the plane, just above stalling speed, along side of Highway 99 and wave to cars passing us at 60 mph. The heat from summer thermals didn't help when landing because the plane would tend to balloon when it came over the concrete runway.

Some of us were not used to the heat we experienced that summer at Lemoore. We were told to take salt pills and drink lots of water. There was no shade at the auxiliary fields and the only water tasted awful. From a tripod was suspended a Lister bag full of chlorinated water and a tin cup. We had to drink that stuff to avoid dehydration.

Several student officers planned a weekend get-away to Los Angeles. One officer had acquired a beat-up, used Model A Ford. To avoid Highway 99 we headed west across the valley toward Coalinga. The car was steaming when we pulled into the only service station in town. A thermometer in the shade on the station wall registered 110 degrees. A patch job on the water hoses got us out of town heading south with all of the water containers we could collect. With frequent stops to cool down and add water, we limped into Los Angeles. Chugging down Wiltshire Blvd. we pulled into the circular drive fronting the Ambassador Hotel. Four 2nd lieutenants walked in pretending we always stayed at the Ambassador. The only accommodation available was a suite. We took it and split the cost. We tried the bars and the Coconut Grove. In one of the hotel bars George Murphy, the dancer, actor, and much later US Congressman, sent drinks to our table. We had a great weekend!

Back at Lemoore AAF we finished our Basic Training in September. I had logged 29:15 hours in the BT-15 and 40:45 hours flying the AT-17, including 10 hours on instruments and 8 hours night flying. I would be heading north, but still in central California, for Advanced Flight School.

Advanced

Still in the class 43-K I reported to Advanced Flight School at Stockton AAF on the outskirts of Stockton, California. We were scheduled for further training in the AT-17 but first had to pass another physical examination. The flight surgeon pulled five of us out of line and told us that it appeared we had a tendency to develop a pileonidal cyst at the coccyx (or tail bone). They thought that long flights in a bucket seat of an airplane could cause problems. Therefore, we were all scheduled for surgery to correct the condition. Because of the operation we were put back one class to 44-A.

On the first day we reported to the flight line my instructor, a 1st lieutenant, took us each up for an orientation ride in an AT-17. He told me to watch him closely and follow him through as he shot two landings. He then asked if I would like to try one. I said I would like to try one very much and took over the controls. As they say, "I creased one," landing without a bump. He suggested that I try another landing. The same result, actually a better landing than he had made. He looked at me and asked if I had been in an AT-17 before. I explained that I had 40 hours in the AT-17 at Basic Training. After a few sharp expletives from the lieutenant, he asked why I hadn't told him that I had been checked out in the AT-17. I told him that I assumed he had checked the flight log of his students. After that we got along great. He was a good instructor and I was the only student in his flight with prior time in the Advanced Training plane.

At Stockton I flew both the AT-17 and the UC-78. They were really identical aircraft built by Cessna, except for some small equipment differences. During Advanced Training I logged a total of 121 flying hours and made 158 landings. Night flying time totaled 21 hours, instrument flying time was 20:05 hours and I put in 10 hours in the Link Trainer. Before graduation I successfully passed the instrument flight test, even though part of my dual instrument time was with a fellow student officer we called "Shoeless Joe." He was a 2nd lieutenant graduate of West Point and proud of the fact that he had the lowest grades in his class and that it had taken him five years to get through the Point. His appointment to the Military Academy may have been due to his birth into a family of southern politicians. Although a very pleasant fellow, Shoeless was very lackadaisical about flight training. When we practiced instrument flying, with one pilot under the hood, it was required that the other pilot stay alert and on the look out for other planes to avoid a mid-air collision. One flight after I had been flying for about 30 minutes under the hood, I pulled the hood back to see Shoeless Joe in the right seat with his eyes glued to a comic book. I told him that if he ever pulled such a trick again, I would report him to the chief instructor. I don't know if it's true, but I heard later that he had killed himself flying an A-20 Havoc in Transition School in Colorado.

In early December, weather in the Stockton area could be bad for flying because of fog. I recall the stories of a couple of cadets making emergency landings due to the weather. Both were on night flights. One cadet looking for Stockton AAF saw a row of lights, thought they were the runway lights, and landed the AT-17 in a large parking lot next to a warehouse. He could not take off the next day and they retrieved the plane with a truck. Another cadet wasn't so lucky. He was up one night when Stockton field closed down due to fog. At low altitude hoping for a sight of runway lights, he spotted headlights of some cars. He landed the plane on a highway south of Stockton and was doing fine until the road turned. The plane went off the road and flipped over in a ditch. Physical injuries were not serious, but the plane was a mess.

When we accomplished all of our required training at Advanced, just before Christmas 1943, it was discovered by a records check that several student officers had not gone through the altitude chamber while at Preflight School in Santa Ana. Before graduating, all pilots needed to have gone through the altitude chamber. It was decided to take six planes to Santa Ana crewed in part with instructors eager to go to southern California. Leaving a couple of days after Christmas we flew in a formation of two flights of three planes. The lead plane following Highway 99 took us through the Grapevine Pass at low altitude, staying between a cloud deck and the highway. It was getting dark as we crossed over Los Angeles and its impressive carpet of sparkling lights. Our leader thought it would be a good idea to take the formation over the Santa Ana Preflight School and give the cadets a buzz job. We went over the base at low altitude and then headed for the Marine Airfield at El Toro. Approaching the field I suddenly noticed lights in the sky above our flight altitude, as did several others in our formation. We scattered when the lights were seen to be on tethered balloons surrounding the airfield. The lead plane had almost flown straight into the balloons. That ill-advised buzz job at Santa Ana could have got us all killed, but fortunately we all landed safely. The next day we went through the altitude chamber at the Santa Ana base and got a short taste of the physical effects of oxygen deprivation.

The plan for a return flight to Stockton the next day was scrubbed. A winter fog blanket had settled in over the northern valley and Stockton. Day after day we got ready to return only to have the flight cancelled by the weather. Finally on New Year's Day, 1 January 1944, we got off the ground. Our flight leader took the six-ship formation over the Rose Bowl in Pasadena. We could look down and see the players on the field. Because the war prevented eastern teams from traveling cross-country the University of Washington was playing the University of Southern California that New Year's Day.

On 7 January 1944 I graduated from Advanced Flight School, got a diploma and an aeronautical rating as a pilot, along with the right to wear pilot's wings. I received orders assigning me to the B-17 Transition School, Hobbs AAF, Hobbs, New Mexico.

B-17 Transition School

Although Hobbs was my destination, there was enough travel time for a detour to visit my family in Del Rio, Texas, before reporting on 22 January 1944. My father, an Army Major, was stationed at Fort Clark, Texas. Generously my parents suggested that I take the family car, a good-looking 1940 two-tone Hydromatic Oldsmobile Coupe to Hobbs. We came up with enough gas coupons for the 350-mile drive from Del Rio to Hobbs.

At the Transition School I was assigned with 33 other pilots (mostly 2nd lieutenants, but a few 1st lieutenants and captains) to Flight M of the Class 44-4-A. It was obvious that we were in for some intensive training. From the light twin engine AT-17 it was a big jump to the heavy four engine B-17 Flying Fortress Bomber.

We had to learn to fly the B-17 in two months. My Form 5 Flight Log shows 29 B-17 flights (some with multiple landings) at Hobbs. Students were required to shoot many practice landings and take-offs. In four days in mid February I made 37 landings. Again in late February I made 14 landings in three days and in March, 12 landings in two days. These were not routine landings. They were touch and go landings with the flight instructor cutting off power on one or two engines before or during final approach. The student pilot had to react immediately with compensating controls and engine power. What really got scary was when the instructor pulled back power or feathered a propeller during a take-off run. During those days of multiple landings I must have lost several pounds from perspiration. We learned what a great airplane the B-17 was, that it could take all kinds of abuse and still keep flying.

When not in the air we spent a lot of time in ground school or in the Link Trainer simulating instrument flight. Also we had to turn out for P.T. to show that we improved in physical fitness. Our total score on tests in sit-ups, chins and two running events had to exceed the score from our previous test.

In local flights we learned to handle the B-17. We found that it was an honest airplane. Both the pilot and copilot had a big control column (about 5 inches in diameter) in front of them with a sturdy half circle control wheel on top. The distinctive throttle controls were designed so that if gripped on top a pilot could control both outboard engines, if gripped on the bottom the two inside engines, and if gripped in the middle all four engines could be controlled with one hand. The arrangement was very helpful for formation flying. The large dorsal fin made the plane very stable; it didn't skid to the right or left. Because of the big vertical stabilizer it was know as an aileron airplane. A pilot had to use ailerons to bank the B-17 to make a turn. Very little rudder control was needed. The controls were not sloppy; you could positively feel the direct reaction of the plane. We learned the rudiments of formation flying at Hobbs, but it took much more practice in Combat Crew Training and with our bomb group to become skilled. More than controlling the attitude of the plane, the big secret to good formation flying was the use of power. The further back your location in a formation, the more difficult it was to adjust to a speed or direction change by the lead plane. Like a string of cars on a freeway, the last car in line has to always make bigger speed adjustments than the second or third car in line. The good formation flyer could maintain his relative position with other planes by subtle changes in his power setting and by anticipating course changes. After a lot of practice it became second nature; one didn't have to think about it and small changes in your plane's relative formation position were sensed as they happened.

While at Hobbs we also participated in several long-distance cross country flights, some at night and on instrument flying conditions. I particularly remember three of these flights, two of which were RON (remain over night) flights. Besides the student pilots and instructors there were usually a radio operator and flight engineer as crew members on these flights.

On one night cross country flight we headed east from Hobbs covering probably 400 to 500 miles on the first leg before turning south, then completing the triangle on a westerly heading back to Hobbs. The instructor had the student pilots take turns in the copilot's seat learning to fly the B-17 at night and working out some navigation problems. It really got quite boring, especially when you were not on the flight deck. When not flying, the student pilots hung out in the nose of the plane or in the waist area trying to keep warm or swapping stories with the radio operator. Shortly after turning back to the west on the last leg I had finished my turn as copilot and went back to the waist to try to get some sleep. About an hour later the radio operator woke me because I was scheduled to go back to the copilot's seat. I made my way across the catwalk in the bomb bay to the flight deck. To signal I was relieving him I touched the left arm of the copilot. He didn't react. His chin was down on his chest; he was fast asleep. Turning to my left I saw that the flight instructor in the pilot's seat was also asleep. No hands were on the flight controls, which I could see were making small corrections on command of the autopilot. I didn't know how long they had been asleep, but the plane was droning along on course and within 100 feet of our assigned altitude. I woke the copilot, took his seat and gently nursed the Fortress back to our assigned altitude. A little later the instructor woke up, looked at me and made no comment. He apparently assumed whoever was in the copilot's seat had been awake while he napped.

In March I went on an RON cross-country to Phoenix, Arizona, in a new silver B-17G. It was the first G model I had been in and it even had a new smell, like a new car. We landed at Sky Harbor Airport in Phoenix. Following a jeep, we parked the big bird near a line of Ryan PT-22 primary trainers. As we were leaving our plane I noticed some civilian pilots walking toward us. In the group I spotted F.A. Allen, my primary flight instructor from Dos Palos. The primary school was being closed and the instructors were delivering the surplus trainers to the desert for storage. They had never seen a G model B-17 with a chin turret. It was with considerable pride that I took my old instructor aboard for a tour of the Fortress. About a year earlier he had taken me up for my first flight.

On take-off from Phoenix the next day our transition instructor asked if we had ever seen the Grand Canyon. A couple of us had not. He put us on a northerly heading and when we neared the Canyon he took over the controls with the remark, "Let's go down for a look." I didn't realize that our instructor pilot was a frustrated "fighter pilot" type. He took that B-17 down into the Canyon just below rim level. What a thrill, but that kind of flying was too dangerous for my blood!

My last cross-country flight was a fortuitous trip to Columbus, Ohio. One day in the ready room with some other pilots, an instructor asked if anyone was interested in going to Columbus, Ohio. I saw a chance to visit my younger brother, a student in the CTD Program at Ohio State University in Columbus, so I volunteered to fill out the crew as copilot. The instructor told me to get my gear and immediately report to the flight line. He didn't tell me that he had not filed a flight plan for the trip. Later I learned that he had a girl friend in Columbus and he had devised a plan to fly to see her.

It was not an unusual weather phenomenon during the winter months for moist air from the Gulf of Mexico to push to the northwest across Texas cooling as it rose in elevation and forming a dense blanket of fog. Hobbs was at 3,600 feet elevation. The instructor must have been briefed by the base meteorologist or knew about the weather patterns. He guessed that the field at Hobbs and others in West Texas would be socked in. We got in the air and flew to the east until he knew the fog had moved over

Hobbs; then he called Hobbs requesting permission to go to an alternate field of his choice until the weather cleared. He got an OK from Hobbs control tower so we headed for Columbus, Ohio, his choice for an alternate field.

We reached Columbus by midday, landed and made arrangements to meet at the airfield the next day. I got a hotel room in town and called my brother. He couldn't get away that afternoon so we arranged to meet that evening. To kill time I walked around downtown, then decided to take in a movie. I don't recall the name of the movie or of the theater, but a billboard advertised a matinee performance by a big band. Inside, the movie was playing when I was ushered to a seat. The movie ended, the house lights came up, the curtains parted revealing a stage full of musicians. Then from the wings, followed by a spotlight, walked Duke Ellington in a white tuxedo. By chance I was able to hear a wonderful musical program by one of the greatest of the big bands. My brother Doug and I got together for dinner that evening. It would be the last time I saw him until after the war.

The next day at the Columbus airport our pilot looked like he had not slept or maybe he had a bad hangover. We got off the ground OK and headed back to Hobbs. Part way we ran into heavy clouds and some turbulence. At the pilot's direction I did most of the flying, logging two hours of exhausting instrument flying time that day. I had passed the instrument flight test on 1 March 1944 so this was good practice.

On 21 March 1944 I completed my last flight at Transition School. I had accumulated 103:45 hours flying time in the B-17.

Near the end of March I returned the Oldsmobile to my parents in Del Rio. It had been a real morale booster to have the use of the car. While there was not very much to do in the town of Hobbs, just to have the freedom to drive into town with some fellow student pilots for an evening relieved the monotony of base life. In the 1940's Hobbs was a town of about 10,000 people and a few paved streets. I recall that there was a brick hotel, The Harden, a movie theater and a couple of cafes. It was hard to raise hell in such a town, but we tried. The only fun we had was crashing some parties given by married officers and their wives.

At the end of our training at Hobbs several members of our class, including me, were told that we were on orders to go to B-29 School at Salina, Kansas. At the last minute those orders were cancelled. Instead we would be going to the Replacement Center in Salt Lake City. From there we would be assigned our air crew and transferred for further training at a B-17 Combat Crew Phase School.

Flight M of my class qualified 34 officers as B-17 pilots. A class photograph was taken when we graduated. Most of these pilots went on to Europe as B-17 air crew commanders. Because of combat losses it is probable that many of those in our class photograph never returned alive to the United States. In the photograph I am fourth from the right in the second row. To my left is Lieutenant Beaugureau and to his left is Lieutenant

Bendedict. I know that these two survived the war. By chance I read an Esquire magazine article about Francis Beaugureau. General Spaatz had heard about his skills as an artist. After Francis had completed his combat tour as a B-17 pilot, the General had kept him in England to paint the air war. A few years ago I learned from the 8th Air Force Museum in Savannah that Beaugureau had given some of his paintings to the museum. I got his address in Arizona and talked to him on the phone. He was still in touch with Bendedict in Florida.

We left Hobbs by train. An engine backed a couple of old passenger cars to a railroad siding on base. With most of our class aboard, the train left for Salt Lake City. After two days shuttling around West Texas and sitting on sidings to allow priority trains to pass, we were about 100 miles east of Hobbs and no closer to our destination. We finally headed north, through the Royal Gorge, and after five days reached Salt Lake City. What a way to run a railroad or a war. With no quarters available at the 18th Replacement Wing we were put up at a downtown hotel while we waited our orders.

Our crew, Number 4805, was activated on 14 April 1944 and we received orders to the 223 AAF BU (CCTS) (H) Dyersburg, Tennessee, leaving Salt Lake City on 18 April 1944.

According to the diploma issued at Hobbs Army Airfield on 24 March 1944 I was a qualified pilot on the B-17 type airplane. Now I would have to prove it to the members of our air crew. Our separate training, our prologue, was over. Supposedly we were now ready for the main event, our training together as a B-17 combat air crew. I was eager to get to Dyersburg AAF and meet the members of our crew.

CHAPTER 1

Phase Training — Dyersburg, Tennessee

Crew assignments were made by the 18th Replacement Wing, Salt Lake City, Utah. The criteria used by the Army Air Force for crew make-up remain a mystery. No two members on our crew were from the same state. Maybe geographical diversity was planned. Our crew was activated on 14 April 1944 as Crew Number 4805. The crew arrived at the 223rd Combat Crew Training School, Dyersburg, Tennessee, on 21 April, except for our navigator, who arrived on 11 May 1944. Combat crew training was divided into three Phase Missions, thus the common usage of the term, Phase Training.

The enlisted gunners were privates first class when they reported to Dyersburg. While going through Combat Crew Training School they were promoted to corporal and later in England with the 381st Bomb Group they were all made sergeants. The flight engineer and radio operator were promoted from corporal to sergeant at Dyersburg and to staff sergeant in England. In April of 1944 a B-17 carried a crew of ten men. By the summer of 1944 the crew size was reduced to nine, with one waist gunner instead of two. The commissioned officers on the crew—bombardier, navigator, copilot and pilot—were all 2nd lieutenants when we arrived at Dyersburg AAF.

Rudy Staszko assumed the responsibility of introducing me to the enlisted crew. He put together a handwritten list describing the civilian background and military training of each crew member. We were strangers and needed to get acquainted. I don't know why or how but there was simply an understanding that we would make this work. I never saw any prejudice, animosity or ill will among members of our crew. We understood that our survival could depend on teamwork. As we got better acquainted, the individual personalities and background differences were complementary and not divisive. Trust and respect came with time as we trained and flew together as an air crew.

The Crew

Tail Gunner – Robert W. (Rob) Whitaker

Rob was born on 23 May 1923. He was 19 years old when inducted on 20 February 1943 from Ripley County, Versailles, Indiana, and entered active service on 27 February in Louisville, Kentucky. He had been working for Western Electric Company as a Toll Telephone and Telegraph Installer. His first posting was to Atlantic City and he then served with the Army

Signal Corps in Missouri. After a day stringing wire, "on his belly,"(Rob's words), he volunteered for Aerial Gunnery School. Before he joined the crew in Dyersburg on 21 April 1944 he was stationed at Joplin, Missouri; Fresno, California; and Gunnery School in Las Vegas, Nevada. Helen remembers visiting Rob at Dyersburg and being impressed when she saw him stand Retreat Parade.

With the 381st Bomb Group, Rob flew 35 combat missions. The tail guns were the most important defense position on the bomber. All gunners must have felt horribly exposed in the tail position of a B-17 because there was no armor plating to protect them from flak fragments. The tail gunner was remote from other crew members. It was not unusual for a tail gunner to squirrel away extra flak vests for protection, a practice Rob had found out about from another tail gunner. We had to convince him that the extra weight of the additional flak vests in the tail of the plane affected its flight characteristics.

I always had the feeling that Rob was more homesick in England than other crew members. He wrote more letters home. I know this because a pilot was required to censor the crew's mail. We all experienced fear in combat, but in addition, Rob felt a strong pull from home and his fiancée, Helen. Yet he would get back in our plane and fly every mission with great courage. I never knew a braver person than Robert Whitaker. I admired him greatly. The crew will not forget his rendition on the intercom of the country tune, "The Great Speckled Bird", when we were back over England from a mission. Rob and Helen spent a week in Seattle with us in 1985, when against his doctor's advice, Rob insisted on attending our crew reunion.

Rob's last combat mission was in early February 1945. He returned to the states by ship. He and Helen were married on 18 March 1945. After R and R in Miami Beach, he was stationed in Laredo, Texas, as a gunnery instructor. When separated from the service on 23 October 1945, Rob was a staff sergeant.

Rob is gone now; he died on November 28, 1992. Helen still lives at their farm home in southeast Indiana near Dillsboro. In 1997 I was able to visit Helen. She took me to Rob's grave at the local cemetery where I tried to say goodbye.

Ball Turret Gunner – David A (Junior) Phillips
Dave was born on 27 July 1925. He was 18 years old when he entered the service on 6 November 1943 at Fort Constitution, New Castle, N.H. His home was, and still is, Kittery Point, Maine. Dave was working in a grocery store after graduating from Traip Academy in 1943 when he volunteered for the Army Air Force. Basic Training was completed at Greensboro, North Carolina, and Aerial Gunnery School at Tyndall Field in Florida.

Although the youngest crew member, hence the nickname "Junior," Dave was mature beyond his years. As a sergeant he completed 35 combat missions with the 381st Bomb Group on 28 January 1945. Departing the UK by ship on 23 February 1945, he reached the USA on 4 March 1945. His discharge came on 26 October 1945.

Reliable, serious, intelligent, Dave quietly did his job. Crew members drew strength from each other. Sensing Dave's ability to conquer fear certainly contributed to our esprit de corps. It took a lot of courage to get into the cramped confinement of the ball turret and ride through enemy attacks feeling exposed to every burst of flak.

Dave had a friend at the 381st, a Sergeant Paul Marston, also from Kittery Point. Paul introduced Dave to a local English couple from Ridgewell—Nellie and Sam Warren. They befriended Dave who used to stay with them on weekends when not flying. Knowing that Dave liked to hunt they arranged for a relative to loan him a gun for hunting on his time off. In November of 1944, Dave obtained a license to carry and use a gun in Great Britain and Northern Ireland.

Typical of Dave, in his letters home to Effie and his parents, he told them that he was still in training so they wouldn't worry about him when in fact he was flying combat missions over Germany. His friend Paul worked at the base camera repair shop. He had been, in civilian life, a photographer for the Portsmouth Herald newspaper. Without telling Dave, Marston sent their picture to that newspaper. The cat was out of the bag. The article with the photo identified Sgt. David A. Phillips as a USAAF air crew ball turret gunner. Another article in that paper reported on Dave's award of a Fifth Oak Leaf Cluster to his Air Medal and that he had taken part in 35 bombing attacks on German targets.

Preceded by his wife Effie, Dave passed away in January of 2001, at age 75.

Waist Gunner – William J (Chick) Collins, Sgt.

Bill Collins is the only regular crew member we have been unable to locate since the war although we have tried to trace him through military records. Reportedly he stayed in England or returned to England to marry a British woman. Bill was older than others in the crew, close to Ellis Richard's age. He had been in the Army Air Force for 13 months when joining the crew in Dyersburg.

In the fall of 1944 the Eighth Air Force changed policy and flew bombardiers only in lead or deputy lead aircraft. Other B-17's in a formation salvoed (or toggled) their bombs on the bomb drop of the lead bombardier's bombs. The crew replacement for the bombardier was called a "Toggleier." He was trained in all of the bombardier's duties, except the use of the Norden Bombsight. This training included the bomb shackling systems, the release mechanism, emergency methods, etc. Bill Collins was selected from our crew to train as a toggleier and flew his last missions in that capacity.

Bill was a very competent airman and could be trusted to always know and do his job. His off-duty exploits were legendary and became part of crew lore. Rudy Staszko relates the following story about Bill Collins. At a pub near our base at Ridgewell, probably the Kings Head, Bill got acquainted with an Irish drinking buddy. One evening the two of them ended up at a cattle auction where Bill bid on and purchased a cow. His plan was to milk the cow so he could drink fresh milk instead of the powdered milk we were given. There was plenty of grass for grazing on the fields surrounding the air field. He got in trouble with the Military Police when he tried to bring the cow on base. They wouldn't permit an aerial gunner to keep a cow. Disappointed, Bill had to return the cow.

Bill was from Pennsylvania. He was a staff sergeant when he completed his combat missions. More of Bill's exploits later in this story.

Waist Gunner – Glenn L. Lamp

Glenn went through crew training in Dyersburg, but was transferred out of the crew when we reached our Bomb Group in England. In the summer of 1944 crew size on B-17's was reduced from ten to nine members, with one waist gunner instead of two. Glenn ended up on another crew; therefore we did not get to know him well.

Radio Operator – Albert D. (Al) Hines

Al entered the service from Ohio in February 1943. He completed Radio Operator's School with the Army Air Force in 1943 and Gunnery School in 1944. He had been an electric welder in civilian life. When he reported to Crew Training School at Dyersburg, Tennessee, Al was about 20 years of age. I had not seen Al for forty years when he came in 1985 to our crew reunion in Seattle. It was a true joy to see him again after those years and to see that he was still the jovial, fun-loving fellow of his youth. Since our Seattle gathering, Al has passed away. His wife, Martha, lives in Canton, Ohio.

At Dyersburg, Al was promoted to sergeant and later in England to staff sergeant. The Training Reports confirm that Al was proficient as a radio operator and gunner. They show nothing of his personality or how he fit in with the crew. While he was skilled at his job, he brought something to the crew we all greatly appreciated—a terrific sense of humor.

Who could come up with an idea to use the bitter cold, up to 60 degrees below zero at mission altitude, to our advantage? Al Hines, the prankster, could. He figured that there must be a way to simplify the very difficult procedure for an airman to relieve himself when on a high altitude mission. The B-17 had what was known as a relief tube, basically a funnel at the end of a hose located in the bomb bay. To get there you had to use an oxygen walk-around bottle. The bulky clothes, pants, electrically heated flying suit, parachute harness, and Mae West didn't help. Used once, the relief tube could freeze and become useless. Al developed a plan. He collected large-sized grapefruit juice cans from the mess hall and put them at strategic locations on the plane. If a crew member had to go, he didn't have to leave his station. He simply used the nearest can. At the extremely cold temperatures the urine froze solid within seconds.

The ingenious part of Al's plan was in the disposal of the cans. He bombed Germany with frozen urine. Before the bomb run the cans of frozen piss were passed to the radio compartment. At "Bombs Away!" Al cracked open the radio compartment door to the bomb bay and tossed the cans before the bombardier closed the bomb bay doors.

He took great pleasure using his secret weapon against Nazi Germany. We all speculated on the effectiveness of his frozen piss bombs. We agreed that the rate of fall would insure that the contents of his can bombs would not thaw out before striking their targets. What did the Germans think about this weapon? Did they think we were running out of real bombs?

Al did a good imitation of some of the popular male vocalists of World War II, sometimes on the intercom. His positive up-beat outlook, his ready smile, his big laugh all helped get the crew through some tense situations.

We valued all the contributions Al made to our crew. We valued his courage and we valued his friendship.

Flight Engineer – Rudolph S. (Rudy) Staszko
Born on 1 January 1923, Rudy was 19 years old when sworn into the service at Ft. Crook, Bellevue, Nebraska, in December of 1942. In civilian life he had been an apprentice machinist. He was sent to Fort Leavenworth, Kansas, for processing, then on to Basic Training at Miami Beach, Florida. Twelve weeks were spent at the Airplane and Engine Repair School at the Curtis Wright Technical Institute at Glendale, California. He passed through Air Force bases at Santa Ana and Fresno, California, before being sent to Washington State College (now University) at Pullman, Washington, for C.T.D. After two months in Pullman he ended up back at Santa Ana Pre Flight School. The Army Air Force decided his skills were more valuable in the aircraft engineering field and sent him to Airplane and Engine Repair School in Amarillo, Texas, for 18 weeks. He then went on to Aerial Gunnery School in Las Vegas, Nevada, before reporting to Dyersburg on 21 April 1944.

Rudy flew 32 combat missions with the 381st Bomb Group. His last mission was on 3 February 1945, a maximum effort raid on Berlin, (the big B). By comparing our mission lists, I believe we flew in the same plane on 28 of Rudy's 32 missions. He was promoted to staff sergeant while in England with the 381st B.G.

Rudy was the glue that held the crew together. The flight engineer was considered the senior non-com on a flight crew. He took his responsibility seriously but with good humor. Very reliable, Rudy was willing to tackle any problem that came up. The flight engineer on the B-17 had double duty. He was responsible for monitoring engine performance, flight instruments, electrical systems, hydraulic systems, and oxygen systems and also for manning the twin fifty-caliber machine guns in the top turret—quite a responsibility! I can still picture Rudy leaning forward on the flight deck, between Ellis and me, calling out airspeed on take-off (while keeping his eye on all engine instruments) as we rolled down the runway with a full bomb load.

The enlisted crew men were sent together for R and R at Spetchley Park, a Manor House loaned to the Eighth Air Force, near Worcester. The R and R (Rest and Rehabilitation) Centers were commonly referred to as "Flak Houses." At Spetchley Park the crew witnessed a fox hunt. Never one to refuse a challenge from the other fellows on the crew, Rudy, at their instigation, got on a horse. Although he had been raised in Nebraska, Rudy claims that he had never been on a horse before. The photo we have suggests that with limited training in equine skills, he was in full command of the animal.

Rudy returned to the States on the USS General Gordon, a ship transporting the walking wounded back from Europe. After some leave time and R and R in Santa Monica, California, Rudy went to Gunnery Instructor's School at Laredo, Texas. He grounded himself because he felt that the B-17 pilots engaged in reckless flying on training flights. " I didn't enjoy looking up at mountain tops." They sent him, of all places, back to Dyersburg AAF, where he developed film from gun cameras.

Rudy was discharged from the Army Air Force in Lincoln, Nebraska, not far from his home in Omaha. He and his wife, Marg, now live in Mission, Texas

Bombardier – Hugh A.(Spider) Treadwell

Born on 21 November 1921 Hugh was 20 years old when he volunteered in October of 1942, but he wasn't called up until January 1943. He had been working in an Oklahoma City bank. His basic training was at Shepard AAF, Wichita Falls, Texas. From March to May of 1943 he went to Texas A and M under the ASTP program. He then went to Cadet Pre-Flight School at Ellington Field, Houston, Texas. During his training, appendicitis got him excused from the physical education program. In true military fashion (SNAFU), he was subsequently given the top athletic award. To Hugh's embarrassment, his hometown newspaper was notified of the award. Bombardier School followed at Big Springs, Texas, from September 1943 to January 1944, when he got his 2nd lieutenant bars. He completed Aerial Gunnery School at Laredo, Texas, in April. On14 April 1944 at the 18th Replacement Wing, Salt Lake City, Utah, he received his crew assignment and reported to Dyersburg, Tennessee, on 21 April 1944..

After gaining combat experience with our crew in England, Hugh went to Lead Bombardier School. He then flew with other crews of the 381st Bomb Group. He was crossed trained as a navigator. By certificate signed by our Group Commander, Colonel Leber, Hugh was converted to navigator. His last and 31st combat mission was to Bremen, Germany, on 30 March 1945. On 13 May 1945 a Liberty ship deposited him in New York. He was then a 1st lieutenant.

Hugh drew some very rough missions over Germany. The lead plane he was in received extensive battle damage and casualties. On a mission with our crew a piece of flack hit him on the chest but didn't penetrate his flak vest. He got right back over the bombsight.

It is possible that Hugh hoped that his wide interest in cultural pursuits might rub off on me. In London he persuaded me to go to a French movie, although I didn't understand a word. To the dismay of other moviegoers, he whispered a translation of the dialog at appropriate times. We did the highlights of London together—Parliament, Buckingham Palace, 10 Downing Street, Westminster Abbey. His knowledge of choral music convinced a sexton to give us a private guided tour of the Abbey.

The Regent Palace Hotel, just off Piccadilly Circus, was our headquarters in London. On one leave we dined to the music of a string quartet in the elegant oval dining room of the Regent Palace. I remember being served by a distinguished elderly waiter who carried a silver service to our table. Lifting the cover he served us macaroni and cheese. Because of rationing, that was the only food on the menu. We had no other choice.

On a less cultural level, when the pubs closed, we were able to gain entry into a few of London's late nightclubs. The clubs were gathering places for the military of all of the Allied Nations. The British appreciated Hugh's droll sense of humor and the Free French officers enjoyed his French with an Oklahoma accent.

Hugh and his wife Edith make their home in El Paso, Texas.

Navigator – Eugene L. (Gene) Nelson
Gene was born in 1921 on the Peninsula north of Green Bay, Wisconsin, near Ephraim on a farm that his grandfather had homesteaded. His career in the Army Air Corps started in October 1942, when he joined the Enlisted Reserve. He had been working as a tool designer for Mercury Outboard Motors in Cedarburg, Wisconsin. The owner and founder assured Gene that he could get an exemption from the draft. He passed all the tests for the Air Corps except for the physical exam. He was underweight. A sergeant told Gene to come back in a week for another physical but to eat five pounds of bananas on the day of the exam. It worked and he was accepted by the Air Corps Reserve. The following January Gene was ordered to report to the 6th Army Corps Headquarters in Chicago. After goodbyes to his family and fiancée, Eunice, he went by train to Chicago, reporting in on January 18th. After a day of mental testing and another physical exam he was assigned to a group of prospective aviation cadets. After four days of train travel, the warmer winter weather made it apparent that they were in the south. On the 5th day they recognized the Jacksonville, Florida, RR Station. They ended up in the Miami area at Biscayne Bay.

After being issued ill-fitting G.I. clothing and getting required immunization shots, Gene spent six week in basic training at the Beach. The group was reclassified as aviation students and shipped to West Virginia University in Morgantown for 12 weeks of exhaustive training in Piper

Cubs. Then on to the Air Corps Classification Center at Nashville, Tennessee, where Gene had another problem with a physical exam. One flight surgeon said that a heart condition would wash him out. On re-examination the head surgeon said nothing was wrong with his heart. Although he wanted to be a navigator, Gene was selected for pilot training and sent in July 1943 to Maxwell Field, Montgomery, Alabama, for Pre-Flight School. He went on to Avon Park, Florida, for Primary Flight Training in PT-17 Stearmans. When Gene had about 20 hours in the air, word came down that qualified cadets could transfer to Navigation School, because of a shortage of navigators in the European Theater; Gene applied and with two other cadets was sent to Advanced Navigation School at Selman Field, Monroe, Louisiana. After three weeks he got orders for Aerial Gunnery School at Tyndal Field, Panama City, Florida. On Christmas day of 1943 Gene was on a train back to Selman Field. Their final exam lasted about seven hours, involving a simulated mission with pilotage, dead reckoning, and celestial, radio and meteorology problems. Another test on a night flight required a three star fix to determine a heading back to the field.

Gene got his navigator wings and was married in the Base Chapel on 21 April 1944. His flight instructor, Captain Ernie Morin, was Gene's best man and his wife was Eunice's maid of honor. Their honeymoon was a three-day, Delay Enroute, on the way to Lincoln, Nebraska. They caught a train to St. Louis, from there another train to Chicago in a VIP car, then on the North Shore Electric to Milwaukee and on to Cedarburg, Wisconsin. After his return to Lincoln, Gene was assigned to our crew on 11 May 1944 arriving in Dyersburg on 14 May 1944.

What a great bit of luck for a pilot to be assigned a navigator in which one could have complete confidence and Gene was a superb navigator. He assumed the responsibility of his job with no nonsense. His competence was contagious. He set a high standard for himself and the rest of the crew followed that example.

After a few missions with the 381st BG, Gene's skills were recognized by Squadron and Group Headquarters. After nine missions with our crew he became a lead navigator and was taken away from our crew. His last and 30th mission was on 10 March 1945. He had flown many of his missions as lead navigator for the 533rd Squadron, the 381st Group and the 1st Combat Wing of the 1st Air Division. While with the 381st Bomb Group, Gene was recommended for the Distinguished Flying Cross. The award was made on 9 June 1945.

I have included a copy of the diary Gene kept in 1944-1945. After every mission flown he made a brief entry in the diary. His pithy comments on each mission are fascinating descriptions of air combat. For example, "Sept 9-#6-Ludwigshaven-Heavy Flak-Accurate-Ship Shot All to Hell-Roughest Mission Yet."

Gene's older brother Ed was also with the Eighth Air Force. He was a sergeant stationed at 8th Air Force Headquarters at High Wycombe. On leave from Ridgewell, Gene was able to visit his brother and attended Ed's wedding when he married an English girl.

After the death of his wife Eunice, Gene sold his home in Cedarburg and moved to Neshkoro, Wisconsin.

Co-Pilot – Ellis E. (Rich) Richard

Born on 12 December 1915, Ellis was 26 when he entered the service on 10 September 1942 at the Presidio of Monterey, California. He had been working as a clerk for the Santa Fe Railroad both in San Francisco and Stockton, California. He took his basic training in October 1942 at Clearwater, Florida. Problems passing the physical examination held up his application for pilot training. The Army Air Force sent him to Gunnery School at Ft. Myers, Florida. After completing Gunnery School in December of 1942 he wound up at Gowen Field, Boise, Idaho. He didn't realize it at the time, but the Bomb Group at Gowen Field was the 381st, the unit we served with in England in 1944 and 1945. While at Gowen Field Rich finally received his Aviation Cadet appointment. His Air Force Pre-Flight School was in San Antonio, Texas. Pilot Training Schools in the Class of 44-C were Primary at Bollinger, Texas, Basic at San Angelo, Texas, and Advanced at Lubbock, Texas, and took from July 1943 to 10 February 1944 when he was commissioned a 2nd lieutenant. His assignment to the crew (and to Dyersburg Phase Training School) was made by the 18th Replacement Wing in Salt Lake City, Utah, on 14 April 1944.

With the 381st BG Ellis completed 36 missions (plus two aborts). His last mission was on 19 February 1945. I don't know how he pulled it off, but Rich flew home from Prestwick, Scotland, via Military Air Transport. After a session flying for the Ferry Command out of Love Field, Dallas, Texas, he was discharged from the service on Christmas Day 1945.

After about twenty combat missions Ellis was made first pilot and got his own crew. I ended up with a series of copilots after that, but none as good as Ellis. He more than deserved his own crew and promotion to 1st lieutenant. On the day of his first mission as pilot of his own crew, all of our original crew not flying that day turned out to "Sweat out the Mission." Waiting for the Group and our Squadron to return, we kept watching for Rich's plane. The weather was terrible, poor visibility with a very low ceiling. B-17's were coming in individually looking for the field. Conditions were ripe for a midair collision when we spotted Rich's plane as it roared low over the Ridgewell control tower. He banked into the landing pattern and set the plane down. We all went over to the Interrogation Room to welcome him back.

Master of the understatement and with a dry wit, Rich was both Mr. Steady and Mr. Cool rolled into one. He refused to be rattled by anything, even some of my bad landings. He helped preserve our sanity in some stressful situations. Ellis claims he was our oldest crew member. I think Bill Collins was about the same age.

I recall one mission when our squadron formation became scattered on a climb through some dense clouds. When we broke into the clear above the clouds and rejoined the formation, we were on the left wing of the element's lead plane. That meant that Ellis from the co-pilot's seat on the right side would have to do most of the formation flying. We had not expected to be on the mission schedule for that day. Rich was tired and sleepy after a late night at the officer's club. It was not unusual for tired crew members to take what we called "No Doze" pills. The pills were not keeping Ellis wide awake. I told him that because of our new position in the flight that he would have to do most of the formation flying. After a few deep breaths of pure oxygen, the unflappable Lieutenant Richard came fully awake and flew perfect formation for about three hours.

Aside from the respect we had for Ellis, the crew and I envied his worldly ways with the opposite sex. Suave, with probably more French blood in his veins than he admits, Rich appeared to take London by storm. I remember one night we had agreed to meet at a late night London club. Of course Hugh and I had struck out trying to find dates for the evening. In walked Ellis with an attractive blonde on his arm. He had met her at Shepard's Pub, a gathering place for Allied service men and their dates. She had probably arrived at Shepard's with someone else, but she left with Rich. He introduced her as "The Duchess." We never learned her real name, "The Duchess of Darby Street."

Ellis and his wife Robin live in Sonoma, California.

Pilot – Edward C (Ed) Carr

I was born 4 April 1922 in Tacoma, Washington. While in high school I falsified my age in order to join the Washington National Guard, the 148th Field Artillery of the 41st Division. My plans were to go to college after high school. However, the National Guard was federalized on 16 September 1940. We were sent to Fort Worden, Port Townsend, Washington, as part of the 248th Coast Artillery Regiment of the Harbor Defenses of Puget Sound. After being promoted to corporal on 6 February 1941 and sergeant on 13 September 1941, I was placed in command of an AA and Seacoast Searchlight crew. Everyone remembers where they were on 7 December 1941 when Pearl Harbor was attacked. The night before is clear in my memory. With some friends we were dancing and listening to the music of the Gene Krupa band at the Century Ballroom in Tacoma. December 7th, the Sunday the war started, the radio requested that all military personnel should immediately report to their base.

On 3 April 1942 I was selected for Class No 2 of the Coast Artillery OCS at Fort Monroe, Virginia. Commissioned a 2nd lieutenant on 7 August 1942, I was made a temporary instructor at Fort Monroe before being sent to San Francisco to await overseas orders. After three wonderful weeks in San Francisco living at the Bellevue Hotel on Gary Street, I was sent with other 2nd lieutenants to Fort MacDowell on Angel Island in San Francisco Bay. We were put in charge of about 500 draftees from the

Midwest on their way to Hawaii for Basic Training. The SS Jane Adams, a Liberty ship on its maiden voyage, took 14 days in convoy to reach Honolulu. All of the 500 draftees were seasick. On 20 October 1942 I reported to Captain Kuhn, Headquarters Battery, 16th Coast Artillery Regiment at Fort Ruger, Honolulu, Hawaii. Tough duty! Fort Ruger was located at Diamond Head, walking distance to Waikiki Beach. I attended the Seacoast Artillery Gunnery School, Fort Kamehameha, graduating 12 December 1942. The captain appointed me the Searchlight Officer of the Harbor Defenses of Honolulu.

Getting transferred to the Army Air Force from the Coast Artillery was part luck, but mostly due to a working knowledge of the "Old Army Game," that is, working the system. Another graduate of my OCS class and my roommate at Fort Ruger was 2nd Lieutenant Ted Gilbert. I believe we were the first 90-Day Wonders to report to the 16th Coast Artillery, a regular army unit. Ted, with administrative skills, was appointed adjutant to the Commanding General. In the fall of 1942 a directive was received from Army Headquarters requesting applications for transfer to the Air Force for pilot training. Two officers would be chosen from all Hawaiian Seacoast Artillery Command applicants. Because of numerous casualties in the fighting on Guadalcanal in October 1942, there was an urgent need for reinforcements. Coast Artillery 2nd lieutenants were being sent to Scoffield Barracks for an Infantry training course, then shipped to Guadalcanal as short-lived platoon leaders. To escape the Infantry and jungle warfare, we devised a plan. Both Ted and I would submit applications for transfer to the Air Force. To make our selections more certain Ted would pigeonhole the requests for applications at Coast Artillery Headquarters only releasing the request to other units so near to the deadline that only our two applications would be received on time. Ted slipped our application forms in with other routine papers for the General's signature. We were both selected and returned to the mainland on the liner Matsonia arriving in San Francisco 17 March 1943 in time to report to the Army Air Force Pre-Flight School in Santa Ana, California, in April.

I had never before been in an airplane, had no burning desire to fly, but knew that the Air Force would be better than the Infantry. Both Ted and I went to Primary Flight School at Eagle Field in Dos Palos, California. Unfortunately Ted washed out of Primary Flying School. I never heard from him again. Presumably he was sent back to the Coast Artillery, but I hope not to the same unit in Hawaii. The Commanding General suspected that there was something unusual about our transfer and he resented being out-maneuvered by two shavetails. Ted certainly deserved to stay out of the Infantry and to survive the war. Our selection for pilot training was not because we were the best applicants, but because we were the only applicants.

From May through December of 1943 I was in pilot training as a student officer. Primary training was in Ryan PT-22's at Eagle Field, Dos Palos, California. Basic was in Vultee BT-15's (the Vultee Vibrator) at

Lemore AAF, California and Advanced in Cessna AT-17's at Stockton AAF, California. From 17 January to 24 March 1944 I was in B-17 Transition Training at Hobbs AAF, New Mexico. I lived in a Salt Lake City hotel from the end of March until 18 April 1944 waiting for an assignment from the 18th Replacement Wing. Crew assignment orders were received on 19 April 1944 and I left for Combat Crew Training in Dyersburg, Tennessee.

In England while flying 35 combat missions with the 381st Bomb Group I was promoted to 1st lieutenant. My last mission was on 14 February 1945.

On 19 February 1945 I left Ridgewell for a Personnel Center near Liverpool and returned to the U.S. on the New Amsterdam docking in New York City 17 March 1945 (exactly two years to the day from my return to San Francisco from Hawaii.) Following some leave in Waco, Texas, visiting my parents I reported to the Santa Ana, California, Processing Center and received an assignment to the ATC Ferry Command at Love Field in Dallas. Because of points accrued from length of service and overseas time, I was granted early separation from the service at Fort Sam Houston, in San Antonio, Texas, on 26 May 1945. My terminal leave expired on 11 July 1945.

After the war I stayed in the Air Force Reserve, retiring in 1970 as a lieutenant colonel. I now live near Port Townsend in Washington State.

Combat Crew Training

Dyersburg Army Air Field was not an impressive air base. It had a very temporary look and feel. Our quarters were of tarpaper construction. It didn't help that May and June were very hot and humid. We were not far from the Mississippi and its backwaters. The town of Dyersburg of about 10,000 folk did not appear to this northerner as a prosperous community. The nearest city for any excitement was Memphis, seventy-seven slow bus miles to the south.

After finishing our training at Dyersburg in June we would be, according to the Army Air Force, a qualified combat-ready B-17 aircrew.

Our Pilot and Co-Pilot Training Reports show we had completed 29 formation-flying hours, of which 21 hours were over 20,000 feet. Assuming we split the time evenly we had less than 15 hours each of actual formation-flight training. Rich, our copilot, believes these training reports are vastly inflated, that our actual formation time was much less, particularly on oxygen over 20,000 feet. I agree. I recall we had to abort an early formation practice because we lost an engine, had to feather a propeller and return to base. What the Training Reports do not show is that had we followed orders we would have left for overseas with a copilot who had never landed a B-17. A training directive required that the first pilot was to be at the controls for all landings. Presumably this practice would improve the air base safety record. We ignored the order. Most pilots did.

How did the Army Air Force choose who was to be the first pilot (thus the airplane commander) or a copilot? First, flying skills did not enter into the equation. Timing was a factor, being in the right place at the right time, as well as length of service, plus just plain luck. The big push was on in Europe. Replacement crews were needed. I had completed flight school in December 1943. Ellis finished flight training in March 1944. His pilot training had been delayed. He had trouble passing the physical examination the first time he applied for pilot training. When that cleared up he had been sent to gunnery school. When he reapplied, the army then claimed that he was too old for flying school. Through some diligent correspondence with an officer he had befriended at the Replacement Wing in Salt Lake City, Rich convinced the Air Force that he was within the age limit when he first applied. He was belatedly accepted as a Flight School Cadet. I had three months B-17 Transition School before reporting to Dyersburg. Rich had never flown a B-17.

Another consideration was length of service. The military had always emphasized longevity in the selection process. I had been in the army since 1940. My date of commission as a 2nd lieutenant was 7 August 1942. I went through flight school as a 2nd lieutenant student officer, not as a cadet. The additional time in grade as a lieutenant gave me longevity and a leg-up for selection as the pilot for our crew.

The Phase Training Reports for the crew and for each crew member show the minimum training requirements set by the Second Air Force and what we accomplished. How accurate are these reports? The big push was on in Europe and the Eighth Air Force needed replacement crews. I suspect that the Training Command was told not to hold back air crews on a training technicality or deficiency.

Since we were being trained to deliver bombs on enemy targets, bombardier training was critical. The Phase Training Reports show that Hugh Treadwell, our bombardier, had 62 practice bomb releases over 20,000 feet and 74 C-1 or A-5 releases. I am certain that we did not make 62 bomb runs over 20,000 feet or at any altitude. Maybe if we dropped a salvo of bombs they counted each bomb as a release. C-1 and A-5 releases must refer to dry runs or to the use of the bombing simulator at Dyersburg. The simulator is difficult to describe. Inside a large hangar was a scaffolding-type rig on wheels. Mounted on top and to the front of this Rube Goldberg-like device was a Norden Bombsight. Placed on the floor of the hangar was a to-scale duplication of a ground target area. An electric motor moved the structure across the hangar surface and over the target mat at a speed simulating, and proportional to, the ground speed of a B-17 at altitude. The Norden Bombsight controlled the steerable wheels on the rig as if the sight was linked to the autopilot of the plane on an actual bomb run. Thus a bombardier could "fly" the rig to the proper bomb release point. Hugh got me into this simulator one day. It was great fun to fly a bomb run inside of a building. To complete this 1944-style "virtual reality" bomb run would have required simulated bad weather, turbulence and pretend anti-aircraft shells.

Gene Nelson's Phase Training Report shows he had 16.2 D/R (dead reckoning) training hours and 9 hours celestial navigation. We all felt that Gene was a complete master of his subject. I am sure he was. He ended up as one of the lead navigators with the 381st BG. He also knew the one critical rule of navigation—the Navigator's Creed. Never ever tell the pilot that you are lost, that you don't know where you are. Gene never did. What a navigator! He reported to Dyersburg three weeks after the rest of the crew.

Our gunners, radio operator, flight engineer, as well as the bombardier and navigator, were required to fire 200 rounds, air to air, from the 50 caliber machine guns when flying above 20,000 feet. The Phase Training Reports show that we had two air-to-air missions (firing at a towed target sleeve) and three air-to-ground training flights. We may have been scheduled for three air-to-ground missions, but I think we only flew one. It was an unforgettable day. How a gunner firing a 50 caliber machine gun from a low-flying B-17 at a stationary ground target could simulate the skills needed to aim and fire at a German ME 109 fighter closing at over 400 MPH is beyond reason. The gunners were required to fire a minimum of 400 rounds to complete their training in B-17's. No one saw any value in the training exercise. We had to fly a rectangular pattern, dropping down to a very low altitude as we passed the target. It was located in a swamp not far from the Mississippi River. A slow airspeed was needed so that the gunners could fire as we passed the target. It was hot and humid, poor flying conditions. The pilot was continually fighting rising thermals over farm fields then sinking over the swamp water. If a crew returned to base with any ammunition still aboard they were sent out again. To avoid that possibility there was an unwritten rule. If the required rounds were not expended through the guns, left over belts of ammo were tossed out of the waist window into the swamp.

Rudy remembers seeing that Hugh Treadwell, our bombardier, was firing very short bursts from the nose gun. He crawled into the nose compartment and held the trigger down as Hugh was beating him on the back. The tracers were making a corkscrew pattern from the free-swinging machine gun. Unless one is considering mining for lead I would advise against investing in real estate in an area west of Dyersburg, near the Mississippi.

So that the air to ground gunnery practice was not a complete waste we took the opportunity, while still at low attitude, to give a buzz job to a river boat before returning to base. Rudy's memory of the event is that he got into the copilot's seat when Rich went to the rear of the plane for a drink. Rich claims he would not have left his seat for that reason. Maybe he wanted to use the relief tube, located in the bomb bay. I think he left his seat to go to the waist of the plane so that he could relive his gunnery days and fire the 50-caliber at the ground target on our last pass. Rudy was in the copilot's seat flying south over the Mississippi. He kept dropping down until I realized that he intended to buzz a ship on the river. It was, as I recall, a bulk cargo carrier of some type. I took over the controls as we passed over the ship a few feet above river level. The boat's crew was on the deck waving their arms as we roared over.

I was called on the carpet at Dyersburg, not for buzzing the ship on the Mississippi, but for a breach of military courtesy by one of our enlisted crew. He had failed to salute a 2nd lieutenant ground officer. The AAF Officers Candidate School turned out administrative officers, referred to by aircrews as "Ground Pounders." Some were very impressed with their new gold bars. I went into the squadron office to hear the complaint. A 2nd lieutenant in a spotless, starched uniform sat behind a desk. Assuming that I had been commissioned a few months before arriving at Dyersburg, he asked why I didn't stand at attention and salute him. Before I replied to this nonsense a thought crossed my mind. Since I was commissioned in 1942 I was probably senior to this guy. I asked for his date of rank and told him that I saluted senior officers and that from now on I expected him to salute me. Also I advised him that I would deal with military courtesy issues on our crew, not him. We had no further complaints.

We did manage to get away from the Dyersburg base a few times. Rudy took a three-day pass to Omaha and spent all of his time traveling. Hugh Treadwell, our erudite bombardier, convinced me to accompany him to town on Sunday for a Protestant church service, a Baptist church I think. Having been raised a Catholic, I had never been inside of a Protestant church. All of the hymn singing was a revelation. Hugh had a great voice, singing with gusto, as I mouthed the words. I am sure that I had a need for some spiritual uplifting.

Some off-base pursuits were other than religious. Hugh and I went on pass to Memphis. Somehow we managed to get dates for dinner and dancing on the roof garden of the Peabody Hotel. The fanciest place in Memphis, the Peabody was a meeting place for Air Force officers. The management of the hotel was not happy the evening that one of our flight officers, with too much to drink, tried to go for a swim with the white swans in the lobby fountain pool. To protect the swans, he was rescued from the pool by the hotel staff.

Bill Collins was our oldest enlisted crew member. In the air he was very mature and reliable. He was more experienced, had "been around" more than the rest of the crew. Occasionally, when looking for a good time, Bill took off on his own. When on leave the crew tended to look out for one another. They would try to keep each other out of trouble and be sure no one overstayed leave time. One night in Dyersburg, Collins disappeared. Knowing he had been drinking, a search was started. According to Rudy Staszko, someone from another crew found Bill sleeping it off in a hen house or chicken coop. From then on Bill was "Chick" to the rest of the crew.

I don't think any of us were sorry to be leaving Dyersburg. However, a song can instantly bring me back over fifty years to the mess hall at Dyersburg Army Air Field. A jukebox in the mess hall seemed to play only one record over and over and over: "I'll Be Seeing You " sung by Dinah Shore. A real wartime tearjerker of a song; but fortunately, we would not be seeing Dyersburg again.

In seventy-five days, on 29 June 1944, we had completed the three phases of our combat crew training. At Dyersburg I had logged about 130 flying hours, some instrument flying and some, but too little, formation flying with the crew. Because of an ear infection, I was grounded the last week of our training.

We were young, we were cocky, and we were a B-17 aircrew. In 1944 the wings pinned on an airman's chest gave him status. Removing the grommet from our hats to give them the 50-mission crush was part of the image; it said we were Army Air Force fliers and set us apart from other branches. As aircrew members we were expected to be a little unmilitary and we tried to meet such expectations.

On completion of our training at Dyersburg, we were declared qualified for combat. If they were going to trust us with a quarter of a million dollar airplane, the Air Force must have thought we were ready. They put us on a train for Kearney, Nebraska.

CHAPTER 2

Stormy Weather

Kearney AAF to Grenier AAF (1450Miles)

We reported to Kearney AAF in Nebraska on 1 July 1944. Crews arrived from several Crew Training Schools to pick up aircraft for overseas flights. In the spring and summer of 1944 most B-17's were sent from the manufacturer to the Army Air Force Modification Center in Cheyenne, Wyoming, then on to Kearney Army Air Field or Grand Island Army Air Field, both in Nebraska. Boeing in Seattle built most of the 12,73l Flying Fortresses, although several thousand were made under contract by Lockheed-Vega and Douglas Aircraft Co. in California. Top production rate was reached in April of 1944 when Boeing was rolling out 16 aircraft per day.

About a day after reporting in at Kearney I was called to the operations office. They had been looking for a crew with a pilot from Washington State. My hometown was listed as Tacoma, Washington. A new B-17 called "Five Grand" had just been delivered to Kearney. The five thousandth B-17 built by Boeing in Seattle had been signed with the names and addresses of the factory workers at Boeing. It was a sight: a silver B-17 with thousands of signatures, many in red lipstick or red markers! The government was considering not sending the plane to combat in Europe until after a select crew took it on a bond tour of the United States. Any reprieve from combat sounded great, as did a tour of many of the major cities and airports in the country.

The next day I was called in again and told that a pilot had arrived who was from Seattle and he would get "Five Grand." Again Tacoma played second fiddle to Seattle. A Tacoman shouldn't have been surprised by this standard favoritism for Seattle. Hadn't Seattle changed the name of our mountain? School geography books in Tacoma clearly identified the mountain as Mount Tacoma. Yet Seattle people ignored such evidence. They said the correct name was Mount Rainier. Retribution came to that Seattle pilot when the bond tour was cancelled. "Five Grand," Serial Number 337716 left Kearney a few days after our departure. It was assigned to the 96th Bomb Group at Snetterton, England, on 14 July 1944.

At Kearney rumors flew fast and furiously from crew to crew. One of the persistent rumors was that an aircrew could make a tidy profit by carrying American whiskey on the flight to England. Bourbon whiskey was not available in wartime England. Reportedly it could be sold for at least $25 a fifth. We were going to cash in. Leave time in Kearney required a stop at the liquor store. Enough bottles were purchased to fill an extra B-4 bag.

The people of Kearney knew that the crews were just passing through enroute to overseas. They tried to make our short stay a pleasant one. On a beautiful summer day (it must have been the Fourth of July) we were invited by local families to share a picnic in the town park. We had a wonderful feast, fried chicken plus, as could only be prepared by some Nebraska mothers—a great treat and escape from the Army mess.

Several of the crews went to a carnival in town. On one of the rides people were in seats at the end of a cable. The circular ride, turning fast, propelled riders by centrifugal force to a horizontal position. On the ride Rudy's extended foot hit a bystander in the head knocking him over. Not wanting to be left behind in Kearney by a lengthy inquiry he didn't identify himself. As a Nebraska resident before and after the war, Rudy has always thought he should try to check back on the accident to see if there had been a serious injury.

My Pilots Flight Log shows that I made a 2:45 hour flight from Kearney AAF on 5 July 1944. I assume our entire crew was on this flight. It must have been a training flight in the Kearney area, a check flight or a break-in flight of a new B-17. I simply do not recall the flight or its purpose; must have been routine and uneventful.

In preparation for our departure for overseas we were given another physical exam, this one by Processing Surgeon Captain C. D. Catalano of the Medical Corps. All on the crew were declared physically qualified for foreign duty. We were blood grouped and certified as completely immunized against typhoid, small pox, tetanus, typhus, cholera and yellow fever. We were all certified Dentally Class IV, whatever that meant.

Our extra clothing and heavy personal items, like footlockers, would not go by air. They were labeled for surface shipment to our destination. Traveling by ship, it would take many weeks for these items to be delivered to our airbase in England.

Navigation watches were issued to some crew members. We knew things were getting serious when all crew members were issued 45 Caliber automatic pistols. No one, however, explained what we were supposed to do with these weapons. In case we had to bail out or crash land, the bombardier was instructed to destroy the highly secret Norden Bombsight with a 45 slug. But we had ten 45 Caliber pistols, one each. Were the pistols to be used for survival in case of a forced landing in Labrador? Did we need protection from polar bears on the ice caps of Greenland? The Army Air Force couldn't have given us a worse firearm for shooting game. I could not hit a stationary target at fifty feet with a 45 pistol. On arrival in Britain the pistols were immediately taken away from us. The Eighth Air Force knew that the last thing an airman needed in case of a bailout or crash landing in occupied Europe was a pistol. German forces did not look kindly on US airmen arriving with a sidearm. A gun might put one's status as a POW in jeopardy under the Geneva Convention.

We were scheduled to depart Kearney AAF on 7 July 1944 on Shipment No. FP 900-BA under Movement Orders, Heavy Bombardment Crew Number FP 900-BA-33 to overseas destination. Assigned airplane was B-17G number 43-38038. This was a Boeing Seattle-built Fortress. It had been delivered to the Cheyenne Modification Center on 19 June 1944 and to Kearney AAF on 28 June 1944. Orders stipulated travel via military aircraft to Grenier Field, Manchester, N. H. Airport of Embarkation, under control of the ATC (Air Transport Command). In lieu of subsistence, officers and enlisted men were authorized a flat per diem of $7.00 for travel enroute to final destination.

The first briefing for the flight was for an early evening take-off from Kearney on 7 July, arriving at Grenier Field, N.H. in the morning. After we had started getting ready for departure, the flight was cancelled. A line of violent thunderstorms was moving across the Midwest from west to east. The delayed flight plan required us to wait for the storm line to move across Nebraska; then we would take off for New Hampshire. About midnight the thunderstorms rolled through with the type of lightning and rain that only huge cumulo nimbus can produce. Our second briefing took place about 0100 hours on 8 July. The weather officer reported that we could expect to run into thunderstorm activity after takeoff. He suggested that we could try on our easterly flight to pick our way through the storms. It was doubtful that we could fly over the storms because of the extreme heights of the cloud tops. If we couldn't fly through the storm line because of turbulence he advised that the best route would be to try to fly around the southern edge. He thought that the line of storms extended further north than south of our flight path.

Rudy, Rich and I went through the checklist with great care. This was it! We were on our own and on our way. We got off the ground at Kearney around 0200 hours. About an hour later we approached a giant electrical display. Vertical lightning flashes lit up the thunderclouds and the night sky. With no experience flying through such a storm, we approached with apprehension. In training we had been told that by observing the lightning strikes and flying between them a plane could avoid the extreme turbulence of such storms. The B-17 is a very stable aircraft. I thought we should give it a try. As we got to the edge of the clouds, we started rapidly gaining altitude even in level flight. Power was cut back to maintain altitude, but almost immediately we started sinking fast and I had to advance the throttles.

Keeping the plane level in the turbulence was not easy, but what really convinced me to turn back was the display of St. Elmo's fire on the plane. Streaks of static electricity could be seen bleeding off our wing tips. The ends of the propeller blades were throwing off bright electrical charges. In the nose compartment Gene and Hugh watched the display of St. Elmo's fire coming from the propellers. Without saying anything, Gene, as a precautionary measure, snapped on his chest pack parachute. Observing Gene's actions, Hugh thought this was a good idea, but he couldn't locate his chest chute. After a frantic search of the nose compartment, he found the chest pack. He had been sitting on it. I was convinced that this was a foolhardy effort. To continue would endanger the crew and the plane. We did a fast 180-degree and headed back west until out of the storm. After a quick intercom conference with Rich and Gene, it was decided to head north to get around the storm line. After flying on a northerly heading for about an hour, it started to get light. According to our Wisconsin Navigator we passed over La Crosse. Reaching the end of the thunderstorms we headed east again, crossing northern Lake Michigan.

After a nine and a half hour flight of about 1450 miles, we landed shortly after 1300 hours at Grenier Field, Manchester, New Hampshire. Our plane was one of the few to make a non-stop flight from Kearney to Grenier Field on 8 July. Because our crew number was 33 on the shipment order I assume there were at least 40 or 50 aircraft scheduled for that night's flight. Most pilots had followed the meteorologist's suggestion and had tried to fly south around the storms. They found that the storm line extended so far that most all of them had to land and refuel. Operations Personnel at Grenier Field told us that there were B-17's from our flight scattered at various airfields all across the southeastern United States. They came staggering into Grenier Field late in the afternoon. I will never understand why we didn't take off as scheduled, before the thunderstorms reached Kearney, Nebraska. All crewmembers have a vivid memory of the thunderstorms on our flight from Kearney. Our copilot, Mr. Calm, says the flight was ok except for the lightning and thunder, which frequently woke him up.

CHAPTER 3

Lost over Labrador

Grenier Field to Goose Bay (950 Miles)

Processing for overseas shipment from the Air Port of Embarkation, Grenier Field, Manchester, N.H. began shortly after our arrival on 8 July 1944. On that date Secret Orders were issued (Movement Orders from Kearney had a Restricted Classification) directing that we WP (will proceed) by air via North Atlantic Route to the European Theatre of Operations, London, England. The specific details of the route would be covered in our briefing. The orders prohibited the sending of safe arrival telegrams while in route and at domestic or overseas destinations.

All crew members were issued winter flying jackets and trousers and sunglasses. Ellis remembers being issued a sewing kit. A friend of his from flight school started the "Thimble Club" at Grenier Field. Using the thimble from the sewing kit he would display it on the end of a finger. If you couldn't reciprocate by showing your thimble, you were supposed to pay a dollar. On 9 July we were briefed for departure to Goose Bay, Labrador. Large bags of mail and C Rations for the American Forces in Europe were loaded in the bomb bay. The plane had been refueled; we were ready to go. Checklist completed we started engines, taxied from the hard stand and turned into the line of aircraft on the perimeter track. B-17's and B-24's in turn would swing onto the assigned runway and on clearance from the control tower would roar past us on their take-off run. We were first or second back in line from reaching the head of the runway when a B-24 Liberator roared past us on the runway. I was watching him out of the pilot's left window as he went by. He seemed to be using lots of runway without getting airborne. I heard a long rumbling noise. Looking back to my left off the end of the runway I saw a black cloud of smoke rising from the ground. A radio message from the Control Tower cancelled any further flights for the day. We were instructed to return to our assigned parking spots and leave the aircraft. Nerves on edge we taxied back and killed the engines.

No one explained what happened to the B-24. Was it overloaded? Did it lose power or an engine on take-off? There were many rumors. One claimed that the plane had struck an MP jeep crossing the end of the runway on the perimeter track. The cause of the crash was probably not determined until much later. That old standard, pilot error, was our best guess at causation.

The accident was still on our minds at briefing the next morning, 10 July 1944. We were told that navigation to the airfield at Goose Bay would have to be dead reckoning (DR). The radio range station at Goose Bay was down that day. Without the radio signal from Goose, we would be unable to home on the field with our radio compass. The weather forecast was good. About 0800 hours we were again ready for take-off. At the head of the runway, pushing the throttles forward, I ran all four Wright Cyclone engines to full power before releasing the brakes. As always I felt an adrenaline rush when sensing the power under my control. The B-17 really vibrates when held back under maximum RPM, but settles down after brakes are released and she picks up speed. After witnessing what had happened to the B-24, we were taking no chances. Throttles were held full forward until we left the ground and raised our landing gear. We left the ground well short of the end of the runway, climbed to our assigned altitude turning on course for Goose Bay.

It was a beautiful, clear day when we crossed over the mouth of the St. Lawrence River, over halfway on our flight of almost 1000 miles to Goose Bay. As we entered eastern Quebec, we passed the last recognizable checkpoint for a visual fix. Below us and on into Labrador were thousands of lakes, all looking alike, indistinguishable on our maps. In the northern latitudes a magnetic compass becomes less reliable. The B-17 we flew was equipped with what was called a Flux Gate Compass, a more reliable instrument. Without the use of our radio compass our dead reckoning course was critical. Maintaining a proper course depended upon our knowledge of the direction and force of the winds we encountered.

To obtain a more precise wind drift reading, Hugh, our bombardier, volunteered to use the Norden Bombsight to read wind drift. Normally the drift meter would have been used. It is a simple instrument. Viewing the surface through an eyepiece, the observer lines up cross hairs with the path being flown over the ground. Comparing that line with the axis of the airplane shows the degree of crab into the wind the airplane is flying to maintain a heading. The Norden Bombsight, having very precise optics, is a more accurate instrument than a drift meter. Hugh read the drift on the bombsight in compass degrees to Gene Nelson, our navigator. Unfortunately there was a difference in terminology in how a bombardier would read degrees of drift and how a navigator would read drift. Hugh reported a drift to the left of several degrees. On a northbound course that would normally mean the wind was from the east. Actually the winds were from the west. What he was reading was the degree of crab the aircraft was in to maintain its course, not its drift. We corrected our course based on the drift reading and in so doing doubled our error because the correction was applied to the right, not the left. A wrong correction of four degrees could put us eight degrees off course. We continued on, between 6 to 8 degrees off course for Goose Bay. We saw water ahead, clearly open ocean, not a bay. The only way we could be coming to the ocean, according to our maps, meant we were east of the proper course. I asked Gene what was going on. He made some rapid calculations and very calmly gave me a new heading of about 270 degrees. We found Goose Bay, flew to the head of the bay and landed.

Because of the dogleg detour we had taken, our plane, after 7 1/2 hours in the air, was last to land in that day's flight to Goose. No one inquired about our late arrival. Gene assured me that he was never lost. We were off course by many miles, but not lost. Technically he was right. By tracing back to where the drift correction was misapplied to our course, he was able to determine how far to the east we had missed our destination. He got us there. Why argue over terms. To be off course is not to be lost, if you know why you are off course!

We were glad to be on the ground. Both Rudy and Dave kept the Air Transport Command note welcoming Transient Personnel to Labrador's Wonderland. The notes were handed out when we left the plane. Rudy recalls being told that the walls of the buildings on base were one foot thick. Food and sleep were in order. We would be at Goose overnight, leaving for Iceland in the morning.

CHAPTER 4

Precise Navigation

Goose Bay to Meeks Field, Iceland (1500 Miles)

Briefing at Goose Bay for the crossing to Iceland was serious business. We would have a full fuel load for the approximately 1550-mile flight. Weather over the North Atlantic would not be VFR. Part of the way we would likely be on instruments. Tail winds would help, but the flight would cross through a frontal system. Cloud decks might prevent us from seeing much of the ocean. Weather at Meeks Field should be all right on arrival, but closing down later in the day.

If we had mechanical problems beyond the point of no return, there were two emergency airfields on Southern Greenland—Bluey West One and Bluey West Two. A pilot had to make a perfect approach to these airfields because they were located in dead-end fjords. There was no chance for a go-around. If for some reason, navigation error or weather, you couldn't land in Iceland you could try to reach Scotland. It was, however, really at the maximum range of a heavily loaded B-17. Other options were: you could bail out over Iceland or ditch in the sea.

The bombers leaving Goose Bay on 11 July took off at intervals a few minutes apart. We got off at about 0800 hours, made a slow climb to the recommended altitude and set the autopilot on course. Before the seas became obscured, Gene Nelson was able to get some drift readings. He also confirmed our course heading by shooting sun lines.

It was on this flight that I noticed that the metal cap over the hub of the pilot's control wheel appeared to be loose. The aluminum cap with the Boeing logo snapped off in my hand. Inside was a piece of paper with the names and Seattle telephone numbers of two female factory workers at the Boeing Airplane Plant. Over the North Atlantic we had little use for the information. Also Al Hines found a nice scroll, about 18 by 24 inches, which was signed by people at the Cheyenne Modification Center. It had been left behind the radio. Both messages were lost or left on the plane when we delivered it in the U.K.

On this long haul to Iceland we encountered instrument flying conditions. My Flight Log for 11 July 1944 shows we were flying on instruments for two hours. About half way to Iceland, off the south coast of Greenland, Gene got some radio fixes to confirm his navigation plot. Later we found ourselves flying between two cloud layers. With nothing to do but try to keep warm our gunners must have been extremely bored.

The flight crew, pilot and copilot were busy monitoring instruments, the flight engineer keeping an eye on engine readings. The bombardier kept check on needs of the crew while the radio operator scanned his dials for messages. The gunners were passengers, occasionally chatting on the intercom to relieve the boredom. From the cockpit or the nose compartment we had no view to the rear. The flight engineer, when in the top turret, had the best view, 360 degrees of traverse. The tail gunner and the ball turret positions had good rear views, but of course would not be manned on a long non-combat flight.

One of our gunners reported that he had been watching another B-17 to our left rear. He saw it from the left waist gun position. The plane was following at about our altitude. It was nice to have company. Reporting in from time to time, our gunners kept tabs on the other Fortress. The pilot of the other plane identified himself on the interplane frequency. He asked if we were certain of our course heading to Iceland. Gene Nelson advised that we were on the proper heading and I relayed this information to the other pilot. Gene recalls that Rich came into the nose compartment and asked, "Gene, where are we?" Gene pointed to his map with his pencil saying, "We are right here." Rich returned to his copilot's seat but reappeared 15 or 20 minutes later with the same question. He got the same definite answer. "We are right here—on course." Gene suspects that I was sending our copilot to the nose for reassurance about our course. Maybe I was.

The next radio message from the other plane claimed that our course, according to their navigator, was too far to the south and a correction of several degrees to the north was needed. When I asked why he thought we were off course he had no reasonable answer. We were beyond getting a radio fix; celestial navigation was impossible and clouds prevented a drift reading. His navigator reportedly had a feeling that a course correction was needed. This was the worst possible reason for a course correction, but the other plane changed course to a more northerly heading. We could see that B-17 off our left wing getting smaller and smaller as its distance from us increased. It was finally lost from our sight.

Approaching Iceland, the cloud deck below us broke up and we could see the ocean again. We turned on our radio compass. When we got a strong signal from Meeks Field radio, our radio compass needle pointed straight ahead exactly matching our heading. A rumor passed around at Goose Bay had claimed that German submarines sometimes surfaced off Iceland and sent out false radio signals to confuse US aircraft. There was no interference with the strong Meeks radio signal on 11 July. Also our navigation was as good as it can get. A low cloud deck was reportedly closing in over Meeks Field and southwest Iceland. We called the tower for landing instructions and landed, touching down about 1600 after a flight of eight hours.

Several other B-17's came in after we were on the ground, but the cloud deck then moved in closing down Meeks Field. After leaving our plane, we heard the distinctive sound of a B-17 passing overhead in the clouds. The visibility by then was zero. There was no way that plane could find the runway, even with GCA (Ground Controlled Approach). With his radio compass he could home on Meeks Field, which was probably what he was doing plus hoping that he could find a break in the clouds. It was our guess that he would be instructed to bail out before he ran out of fuel. Fortunately a fighter strip not far from Meeks still had slightly better visibility. The pilot spotted the short fighter air strip and was able to get the plane on the ground without damage. The short runway would however preclude a safe take-off of a B-17. A weather system had settled in over Iceland. With extremely poor visibility it looked like we would be weathered in for a few days.

After the long flight we would have preferred food and sleep, but first had to attend a lecture on proper conduct while in Iceland. Many Icelanders were not happy with a United States Air Base on their soil, fearing it would jeopardize their neutrality in the war. The capital, Reykjavik, about 35 miles from Meeks Field, was off –limits. We would be allowed to go to the nearby fishing village of Keflavik. There would be no fraternization with the women of Iceland and we were to be courteous to all locals. Any breach of conduct would result in severe punishment.

The next morning the word spread that we should get out to the landing strip to see the return of the missing B-17. Off the end of a runway we saw a jeep approaching on a dirt road. It was coming across an open field and leading a B-17. What a startling sight to see this lumbering bomber coming through the mist! The sliding side windows of the cockpit were open so that the pilot and copilot could lean out for better vision of the leading jeep. The road was fairly level and was firm enough to support the plane. The outboard engines were used for power and steering along with the use of brakes when necessary. I doubt that any other multi-engine airplane was sturdy enough for such a journey. The B-17 had taxied from the fighter strip to Meeks Field making frequent stops to cool down the engines. Many aircrews assembled near the end of the runway to cheer the pilot and copilot on as they reached the perimeter track. How did they enter all of that taxi time in their flight log?

We spent four rather uneventful days at Meeks Field waiting for the weather to break. Although we were not allowed to send telegrams, letters were permitted, so we wrote home. Our plane was checked over by mechanics. They replaced the vacuum pump on one engine. Rudy remembers that crews were required to have one member stand guard at their plane at all times. He got the duty on the day the rest of the crew got passes and went to Keflavik. In town we anticipated that we would have trouble communicating with the local people. We saw some young boys fishing from the end of a pier. Gene Nelson recalls going into a hardware store with Bill Collins who wanted to buy some fishing gear. Bill found some fishing line and was trying to explain with gestures that he wanted to buy some sinkers for the line. In perfect English the proprietor suggested that he use four nuts in place of regular sinkers. We were unaware that English was a required subject in Icelandic schools. Bill and other crew members had fun with the kids fishing from the pier. They ended up helping the kids cut bait. Dropping lines from the pier the boys, with the crew's help, were having great success pulling in fish. I don't recall if it was day or night when we got back to the base from Keflavik. At 64 degrees North in July it was still light at midnight. Some airmen killed time in the long evening hours playing cards. Ellis says he lost $2.75 at blackjack in Iceland, but this statement could mean that he was a big winner!

CHAPTER 5

A Common/Uncommon Language

Meeks Field to Valley Wales, UK (Approximately 960 miles)

With weather improving in the Eastern Atlantic we were scheduled for a morning take-off on 15 July 1944. Our destination was the airdrome at Valley, Wales. Valley is in northwest Wales, on Anglesey, near the port town of Holyhead on the Irish Sea. This would be a shorter flight than the one to Iceland but on a more southerly heading, we would not have such favorable tail winds. We got off the ground at Meeks Field about 0800 hours, climbed to our set altitude, and took up the heading for the U.K.

The weather was clear, the ocean blue and our flight smooth. Great Britain was a much larger destination than Iceland so navigation was less critical. Around noon, or shortly after, we saw some small boats on the sea. They must have been fishing boats out of the Orkney Islands or northern Scotland. Then we spotted land, islands and more islands. South we went toward the Irish Sea. Scotland was to the east, then the Isle of Skye, Mull, Islay, and then the Isle of Man. Ireland was off our right wing. With such a bonanza of visual reference points our navigator was having a field day with his maps and charts. After 1500 hours we approached Anglesey and Valley, Wales. The airfield was spotted near the town of Holyhead. I got on the radio to the control tower, "Valley, this is Army 038, landing instructions please."

In reply a very British accent, "Army 038, you are clear to land, runway three zebra, don't land short of the <u>chicken market.</u>"

Confused I called again, "Valley, this is Army 038, please repeat landing instructions."

The same British voice, "Army 038, you are clear to land runway three zero, do not land short of the white <u>checker board.</u>"

I try again, "Valley, this is Army 038, don't land short of what?"

"Army 038, the <u>chicken pox!</u>"

I look at Rich; he looks at me and shakes his head. "Pilot to Navigator, Gene, do you understand what he is saying?"

"Navigator to Pilot, sounds like he is saying something like '<u>chicken wire.</u>'"

During this exchange with the control tower, I spotted the assigned runway, took a reciprocal heading on the downwind leg, turned on the base leg and lowered landing gear. But I still did not understand the landing instructions. We turned on to final and I called for Rich to lower flaps. Rudy called out our airspeed. As we started to flare out I saw that the end of the runway was under repair and torn up. Next to the broken concrete area there were white crosses painted on the runway surface: "White checkered marks." I applied power to clear the area, and then cut the throttles and touched down. Rich claims that it was the best landing he had ever seen me make. In silence, he had endured some not so smooth landings. I take his remark as a high compliment. We landed at 1530 on 15 July.

As we taxied from the end of the runway a jeep appeared with a "Follow Me" sign. It led us to the apron where we were given the signal to cut engines. A captain drove up in a jeep and requested that we exit the plane. He asked me for copies of the Memorandum Receipt that I had signed at Kearney, Nebraska, when B-17 number 038 had been turned over to us. That receipt showed that I, a second lieutenant, had signed for a quarter of a million dollar airplane—the exact cost to the penny that the Army Air Force paid Boeing for the plane is shown. Now I was to turn the plane over to the 8th Air Force. I still have the receipt signed by Captain Robert B. Helfrick of Detachment B. Supply Section BAD No. 1 of Valley, Wales, for one B-17G, A/C Serial No. 143-38038 with Confidential Equipment, Radio, and Bombsight. The captain tells us we will be taken to quarters for the night. A truck will remove our personal gear from the plane and deliver it to our quarters.

B-17 Number 038, our home for eight days, had taken us across the Atlantic. In that short time we had developed an attachment to that B-17. The engines had purred along steadily for 32 hours in the air as we covered about 4800 miles. It was a very stable airplane that flew itself when trimmed. According to the book, B-17 The Flying Fortress Story, by Roger Freeman and David Osborne, Aircraft No. 43-38038 was assigned to the 838th Bomb Squadron, 587th Bomb Group (H) at Lavenham. On 19 March 1945 it had a mid-air collision with another B-17 of the same Bomb Group and crashed in Allied territory near Couvron, France. A sad end for that beautiful silver fortress we flew out of Kearney, Nebraska, in July of 1944.

After being fed and checked into our quarters we assembled with other crews to receive our personal baggage from the plane. The baggage delivery system at Valley was a long way from the carousels at a modern airport. An army truck, piled high with duffel bags and B-4 bags backed up outside of our quarters. Two G.I.'s climbed up on the back of the truck and started throwing bags to the ground where they formed a large heap. Some bags missed the stack and thudded onto the concrete surface. One bag landed nearby with a crash of broken bottles. The smell of whiskey filled the air as the liquor seeped from the bag. A quick check identified it was a bag from another crew. Close to panic we stationed crew members around the truck hoping to identify the B-4 bag containing our precious booze. I persuaded one of the G.I.'s to hand some of the bags over the sideboards of the truck. We saved our valuable cargo!

The quarters provided at Valley for the arriving crews dampened the excitement of reaching the end of our long flight. They were very depressing; the rooms resembled concrete cells with one small high window. Jammed-in army cots took up almost all of the floor space in each damp room. What a welcome to the big war. Thank God we were going to be there for only one night!

We had to do something to celebrate our safe arrival in Britain and break the gloom of the place. Someone suggested that we open a bottle and have a drink. Great idea! We opened and passed a bottle around. A friend from another crew stopped by our door. We had to invite him in for a drink. The word got out—Carr's crew was throwing a party! The parade started; they arrived with glasses in hand. We didn't know we had so many friends. On into the evening we kept opening bottles for our guests. Our supply of whiskey and our potential profits steadily disappeared.

We had been told not to leave the base at Valley. The Eighth Air Force did not want crew members disappearing before departure for the Replacement Depot scheduled for the next day. Waist gunner, Bill Collins, was missing from our impromptu party. It was unusual for Bill to pass up a free drink. As the party was winding down in the early morning hours he appeared. Bill had decided to check out the pubs in a nearby village. He met a local girl. They consumed a few pints. She lived on a small farm and she was friendly. He had everyone's attention as he told his story. Bill was holding court. How did they get along? Leaving the pub he had walked her to the farm, but they never got to the house; they stopped in the barn.

The British, in a classic wartime saying, described American Airmen as "Overpaid, Over-sexed and Over Here." True, but the Americans were also quite amazed by the openness and frankness of the British women on the subject of sex. The Music Hall hit of the day and pub sing-a-long song was "Roll Me Over in the Clover. Lay Me Down and Do It Again."

In the barn, the young lady and Bill ended up, not in the clover, but in the hay. Probably much too eager preparing for the encounter, Bill was fumbling trying to put on a condom. The Welch lass, aware of his clumsiness, in a very calm voice said, "Oh, take it off! Let's chaunce it." Her pronunciation of "chance" as "chaunce" struck Bill so funny that his laughter broke the spell of the moment.

The story was told and retold. The phrase, "Let's chaunce it!" became a by-word for our crew. When a decision was needed in a tense situation that might affect the crew, someone invariably would come through on the intercom with "Let's chaunce it!" Returning from a combat mission into Germany, it was touch and go if we had enough fuel to make it across the channel to our base at Ridgewell. Even with a lot of battle damage and only two engines with full power I wanted to return to base, not end up landing in Belgium. I felt that I should tell the crew that there was a risk of ditching in the channel if we tried to make it to England. After my message to the crew, a voice came through on the intercom, "Let's chaunce it!" So we did and made it back to Ridgewell.

After one night in Valley, Wales, we left by train the next day. Our destination was the Replacement Depot at AAF Station 594 at Stone, England, near Stoke-on-Trent.

B–17 Transition School
On the Flight Line at Hobbs AAF, New Mexico 1944

CLASS 44-4-A   FLIGHT M

Graduates • B–17 Pilots School, Hobbs AAF, New Mexico
March 1944
Ed Carr – 2nd row, 4th from right

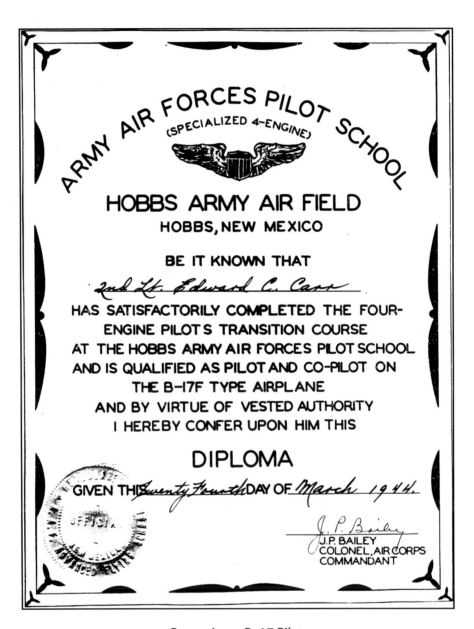

ARMY AIR FORCES PILOT SCHOOL

(SPECIALIZED 4-ENGINE)

HOBBS ARMY AIR FIELD
HOBBS, NEW MEXICO

BE IT KNOWN THAT

2nd Lt. Edward C. Carr

HAS SATISFACTORILY COMPLETED THE FOUR-
ENGINE PILOTS TRANSITION COURSE
AT THE HOBBS ARMY AIR FORCES PILOT SCHOOL
AND IS QUALIFIED AS PILOT AND CO-PILOT ON
THE B-17F TYPE AIRPLANE
AND BY VIRTUE OF VESTED AUTHORITY
I HEREBY CONFER UPON HIM THIS

DIPLOMA

GIVEN THIS *Twenty Fourth* DAY OF *March 1944.*

J. P. Bailey
J.P. BAILEY
COLONEL, AIR CORPS
COMMANDANT

Becoming a B–17 Pilot
24 March 1944

Hugh Treadwell
Dyersburg 1944

Ed Carr
Memphis Leave, 22 June 1944

Standing L–R
Ed Carr, Al Hines
Kneeling
Dave Phillips, Bob Whitaker
Dyersburg 1944

Ed Carr
Dyersburg 1944

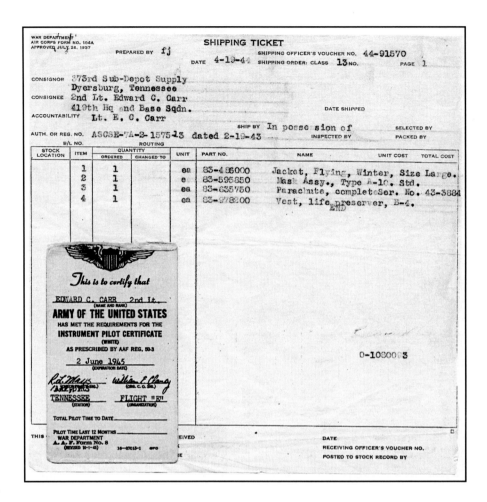

WAR DEPARTMENT
AIR CORPS FORM NO. 104A
APPROVED JULY 26, 1937

PREPARED BY fj

SHIPPING TICKET

SHIPPING OFFICER'S VOUCHER NO. 44-91570

DATE 4-19-44   SHIPPING ORDER: CLASS 13 NO.   PAGE 1

CONSIGNOR 375rd Sub-Depot Supply
           Dyersburg, Tennessee
CONSIGNEE 2nd Lt. Edward C. Carr
           419th Hq and Base Sqdn.   DATE SHIPPED

ACCOUNTABILITY Lt. E. C. Carr

                                    SHIP BY In possesion of   SELECTED BY
AUTH. OR REG. NO. ASCSE-7A-2-1575-13 dated 2-19-43   INSPECTED BY   PACKED BY
B/L NO.   ROUTING

STOCK LOCATION	ITEM	QUANTITY ORDERED	CHANGED TO	UNIT	PART NO.	NAME	UNIT COST	TOTAL COST
	1	1		ea	83-496000	Jacket, Flying, Winter, Size Large.		
	2	1		e	83-595850	Mask Assy., Type A-10. Std.		
	3	1		ea	83-635750	Parachute, complete Ser. No. 43-3884		
	4	1		ea	83-978200	Vest, life preserver, B-4.		
						END		

This is to certify that

EDWARD C. CARR   2nd Lt.
(NAME AND RANK)

ARMY OF THE UNITED STATES

HAS MET THE REQUIREMENTS FOR THE

INSTRUMENT PILOT CERTIFICATE
(WHITE)

AS PRESCRIBED BY AAF REG. 50-3

2 June 1945
(EXPIRATION DATE)

R.L. Mays   William E. Clancy
(ADJUTANT) (SIG.)   (DIR. C. O. SIG.)

TENNESSEE   FLIGHT "E"
(STATION)   (ORGANIZATION)

TOTAL PILOT TIME TO DATE

PILOT TIME LAST 12 MONTHS
WAR DEPARTMENT
A. A. F. Form No. 8
(REVISED 10-1-43)   16-27013-1   GPO

0-1080003

THIS   RECEIVED   DATE

                                               RECEIVING OFFICER'S VOUCHER NO.

                                               POSTED TO STOCK RECORD BY

Dyersburg 1944 · Equiped and Certified

CARR, EDWARD C. 2nd Lt.   O-1080093

Examinations	Class	Date	Signature of Flight Surgeon	Station	Remarks
Qualified for flying	I	4/18/44	[signature] major	AAF, TENN.	None.
Qualified for flying	I	21 Apr 45	J.C. Wilcox capt m	B-4 Serias	Calif
Qualified for flying					
Qualified for flying					

WAIVERS: Coccidiod — Negative 1-18-44

Blood Type "B"	DATES			REACTIONS	INITIALS OF MEDICAL OFFICER
	First	Second	Third		
Smallpox	8-26-42	-/-,	8-44	Immune 2/41 Vaccinoid	CT
Triple typhoid	Complete 9-7-42			Booster 1-18-44 17 Feb '45 CT LR	
Cholera	C-4-27-44	5-4-45 c)		RPM	
Antitetanus	Complete 12-24-41.	Booster 9-28-42 -1-18-44 So 4-19-44	17 Feb 45 RR		
Yellow fever	3-29-42, Lot 380, Amt. .05	None 4-19-44	HTW		
Typhus	C-5-2-44	6-Dec 44 St		RPM LR	
Plague					

10-32808-1

NAME → CARR, EDWARD C.   AERONAUTICAL RATING → Pilot

DATE	STATION	RESULT	DEFECTS	WAIVER	PERSONNEL ORDERS (NO., HQ., DATE)	F/S INIT.
4-21-44	Santa Ana, Calif	I	None	None		

THEATER	DATE ENTRY	DATE DEPARTURE	HOURS FLOWN	ILLNESS OR INJURY	FLYING STATUS
ETO	July 4-44	March 17-45	361	None	FFD

DATE	HQ.	RESTRICTION	DATE REMOVED	ALTITUDE INDOCTRINATION		
				DATE	STATION	TYPE
				Dec. 43	Santa Ana, Calif	I & II

NIGHT VISION → DATE →   RATING →

O-1080093   2nd Lt.   CARR, EDWARD C.

10-41388-2 ☆ GPO

We are Examined, Inoculated and Vaccinated

On leave from Dyersburg.
Hugh Treadwell and Ed Carr with dates at Roofgarden of Peabody Hotel,
Memphis Tn.   May or June 1944

Dyersburg AAB – Barracks
Photo courtesy of DAAB Mem. Association

Dyersburg B–17 (note DY on tail) over Mississippi River.
Photo courtesy of DAAB Mem. Association

198-51

Carr, Edward C.	2nd Lt.	O-10 0093
(Airplane Commander)	(Rank)	(ASN)
14, April 1944	18th RW SLC Utah	4805
(Date Crew Activated)	(Station)	(Number)

FIRST PHASE

Army Air Field, Dyersburg, Tenn.	223rd Combat Crew Training School
(Station)	(Organization)

21, April 1944		25
(Date Arrived)	(Date Departed)	(No. of Days)

First Phase Missions Completed

1	2	3	4	5	6	6A	7	7A	8	8A	9	10	10A	11
C	C	C	C	C	C	C	C	C	C	C	C			C

11	12	12A	13	14	15	16	16A	16B	17	17A	17B	18	18A	18B
C	C	C	C	C	C	C	C	C	C	C	C	C	C	C

SECOND AND THIRD PHASE

Army Air Field, Dyersburgk Tenn.	223rd Combat Crew Training School
(Station)	(Organization)

	29, June 1944	54
(Date Arrived)	(Date Departed)	(No. of Days)

Second Phase Missions Completed

1	2	3	3A	4	4A	5	6	6A	7	7A
C	C	C	C	C	C	C			C	C

7B	8	8A	9	9A	10	10A	11	12	12A	12B
C	C	C	C	C	C	C	C	C	C	C

Third Phase Missions Completed

1	2	3	3A	4	5	5A	5B	6	6A	7
C	C	C	C	C	C	C				C

7A	8	8A	9	10	10A	11	11A	12	12A	13
C	C	C	C	C	C	C	C	C	C	C

SECOND AIR FORCE
PILOT OR CO-PILOT TRAINING REPORT

Carr, Edward C.	2nd Lt.	O-1080093	4805
Name: Cross out one (Pilot)-(Co-Pilot)	Rank	ASN	Crew Number

14, April 1944		18th RW SLC Utah	
Date Crew Activated	Group Pre- 5/43 Prim.7/43	Squadron Easic 9/43 Adv. 1/44	Station Trans. 3/44
359:55			
Total Flying Time		Previous Schools Attended – Dates	

FIRST PHASE

21 April 1944	AAF, Dyersburg, Tenn.	
Date Assigned	Station	Date Transferred to Second Phase

1. Instrument Time — 16:15

2. Formation Time — 7:35

3. Instrument Check (Date Passed) — 5/1/44

4. Number Bombs Released —

5. Proficiency Checks Completed — yes

6. Total Time in Assigned A/C at this Station — 52:50
   84 55
   13 7:45

SECOND AND THIRD PHASE

	AAF, Dyersburg, Tenn.	29, June 1944
Date Assigned	Station	Date Transferred to Processing Station

1. Formation over 20,000 feet — 21:15

2. Other Formation — 21:35

3. Rounds, Air-to-Air, over 20,000 feet —

4. Other Rounds, Air-to-Air or Air-to-Ground —

5. Instrument Check (Date Passed) — 6/2/44

6. Number Bombs Released over 20,000 feet —

7. Number Other Bombs Released —

8. Total Time over 20,000 feet — 36:05

9. Total Time in Assigned A/C at this Station — 84:55

Pertinent remarks by the instructor of this crew member will be noted on back.

SECOND AIR FORCE
PILOT OR CO-PILOT TRAINING REPORT

Richard, Ellis E.	2nd Lt.	O-714568	4805
Name: Cross out one ~~(Pilot)~~ (Co-Pilot)	Rank	ASN	Crew Number

14, April 1944		18th RW SLC Utah	
Date Crew Activated	Group	Squadron	Station
	Pre- 9/43	Basic 1/44	
215 :55	Prim.11/43	Asv. 3/44	
Total Flying Time		Previous Schools Attended — Dates	

FIRST PHASE

21 April 1944	AAF, Dyersburg, Tenn.	
Date Assigned	Station	Date Transferred to Second Phase
1. Instrument Time		2:00
2. Formation Time		7:35
3. Instrument Check (Date Passed)		
4. Number Bombs Released		
5. Proficiency Checks Completed		yes
6. Total Time in Assigned A/C at this Station		52:50

SECOND AND THIRD PHASE

	AAF, Dyersburg, Tenn.	29, June 1944
Date Assigned	Station	Date Transferred to Processing Station
1. Formation over 20,000 feet		21:15
2. Other Formation		21:35
3. Rounds, Air-to-Air, over 20,000 feet		
4. Other Rounds, Air-to-Air or Air-to-Ground		
5. Instrument Check (Date Passed)		
6. Number Bombs Released over 20,000 feet		
7. Number Other Bombs Released		
8. Total Time over 20,000 feet		36:95
9. Total Time in Assigned A/C at this Station		84:55

Pertinent remarks by the instructor of this crew member will be noted on back.

2ND AIR FORCE FORM
· A-303 A (9-1-43)

SECOND AIR FORCE
NAVIGATOR'S TRAINING REPORT

Nelson, Eugene L.	2nd Lt.	O-723149	4805
Name	Rank	ASN	Crew Number

14, April 1944		18th RW SLC Utah	
Date Crew	Group	Squadon	Station
	Pre- 8/43	F.G. 12/43	
107:50	Prim. 9/43	Adv. Nav. 4/44	
Total Flying Time		Previous Schools Attended — Dates	
Prior to First Phase			

FIRST PHASE

11, May 1944	AAF, Dyersburg, Tenn.	
Date Assigned	Station	Date Transferred to Second Phase

1. Date Calibration Mission _____
2. Number Hours D/R _____
3. Number Hours Celestial _____
4. Rounds Fired _____
5. Number of Bombs Released _____
6. Proficient in Pilotage __yes__
7. Proficient in Radio Procedure __yes__
8. Proficient in Radio Compass __yes__
9. Proficient Checks Completed __yes__
10. Total Time in Assigned A/C at this Station __5:20__

SECOND AND THIRD PHASE

	AAF, Dyersburg, Tenn.	29 June 1944
Date Assigned	Station	Date Transferred to Processing Station

1. Date of Calibration Mission __6/3/44__
2. Number of Hours above 20,000 feet __30:05__
3. Number of Hours D/R __16:20__
4. Number of Hours Celestial __9:00__

69

SECOND AIR FORCE
BOMBARDIER'S TRAINING REPORT

Treadwell, Hugh W.		2nd Lt.	0-708027	4805
Name		Rank	ASN	Crew Number
14, April 1944		18th RW SLC Utah		
Date Crew	Group	Squadron	Station	
	Adv. Bomb. 1/44			
97:40	A.G. 3/44			
Total Flying Time Prior to First Phase	Previous Schools Attended — Dates			

Total Releases to Date	C.E.A. Converted to 12,000 feet

FIRST PHASE

21, April 1944	AAF, Dyersburg, Tenn.	
Date Assigned	Station	Date Transferred to Second Phase

1. Releases in Assigned A/C   Combined in

2. C.E.A. Converted to 12,000 feet   2nd and 3rd

3. Number C-1 or A-5 Releases   phases.

4. Hours Acting as Navigator

5. Proficient Checks Completed   yes

6. Total Time In Assigned A/C at this Station   48:30

SECOND AND THIRD PHASE

	AAF, Dyersburg, Tenn.	29, June 1944
Date Assigned	Station	Date Transferred to Processing Station

1. Releases over 20,000 feet   62

2. Number C-1 or A-5 Releases   74

3. Other Releases   23

4. C.E.A. Converted to 12,000 feet   254.4

5. Rounds Air-to-Air over 20,000 feet   200

6. Other Rounds   400

7. Hours Acting as Navigator   12:15

8. Total Time above 20,000 feet   36:05

9. Total Time in Assigned A/C at this Station   84:55

5. Rounds Fired over 20,000 feet   200

6. Other Rounds   400

7. Proficient in Pilotage   yes

8. Proficient in Radio Procedure   yes

9. Proficient in Astro-compass   yes

10. Total Time in Assigned A/C at this Station 68:05

Pertinent remarks by the instructor of this crew member will be noted below.

70

2ND AIR FORCE FORM
A-303 C: (9-1-43)

SECOND AIR FORCE
ENGINEER'S TRAINING REPORT

Staszko, Rudolph S. _____ Sgt. 37469124 4805
          Name   Rank   ASN   Crew Number

14 April 1944 _____   18th RW SLC Utah
  Date Crew   Group   Squadron   Station
  Activated

16:00   A.M. 44
  Total Flying Time   F.G. 44
  Prior to First Phase   Previous Schools Attended — Dates

FIRST PHASE

21, April 1944   AAF, Dyersburg, Tenn. _____
  Date Assigned   Station   Date Transferred
                                             to Second Phase

1. Proficiency Checks Completed   yes

2. Total Time in Assigned A/C at this Station   52:50

SECOND AND THIRD PHASE

_____   AAF, Dyersburg, Tenn. _____   29 June 1944
  Date Assigned   Station   Date Transferred
                                                to Processing

1. Rounds, Air-to-Air, over 20,000 feet   200

2. Other Rounds   400

3. Total Time over 20,000 feet   36:05

4. Total Time in Assigned A/C at this station   84:55

Pertinent remarks by the instructor of this crew member will be noted on back.

SECOND AIR FORCE
RADIO OPERATOR'S TRAINING REPORT

Hines, Albert D.
Name — **Rank** — 35608948 — 4805
ASN — **Crew Number**

14, April 1944
Date Crew Activated — **Group** — 18th RW SLC Utah
Squadron — **Station**

11:40
Total Flying Time Prior to First Phase

R.O.M. 43
F.G. 44
Previous Schools Attended — Dates

FIRST PHASE

21, April 1944 — AAF, Dyersburg, Tenn.
Date Assigned — **Station** — **Date Transferred to Second Phase**

1. Code Speed Sending	11
2. Code Speed Receiving	18
3. Number Air Rounds Fired	150
4. Proficient Checks COmpleted	Yes
5. Total Time in Assigned A/C at this Station	32:00

SECOND AND THIRD PHASE

AAF, Dyersburg, Tenn.
Date Assigned — **Station** — 29, June 1944
Date Transferred to Processing Station

1. Code Speed Sending	15
2. Code Speed Receiving	20
3. Number of Rounds over 20,000 feet	200
4. Other Rounds Fired	400
5. Total Time over 20,000 feet	36 :05
6. Total Time in Assigned A/C at this Station	80:35

Pertinent remarks by the instructor of this crew member will be noted on back.

SECOND AIR FORCE
GUNNERS FLYING TRAINING REPORT

Collins, William J.   Pfc G.l.   33600428   4805
_____   _____ _____ _____
           Name   Rank   ASN   Crew Number

14, April 1944   18th RW SLC Utah
_____ _____ _____
Date Crew   Group   Squadron   Station
Activated

21:05   A.G. 44
_____ _____ _____
  Total Flying Time   Previous Schools Attended — Dates
Prior to First Phase

FIRST PHASE

21, April 1944   AAF, Dyersburg, Tenn.
_____ _____   _____
  Date Assigned   Station   Date Transferred
                                                      to Second Phase

1. Number Air-to-Ground Malfunction Missions   3
                                                      _____

2. Number Times Operated Ball Turret   2
                                                      _____

3. Number Times Operated Upper Turret   13
                                                      _____

4. Proficient Checks Completed   yes
                                                      _____

5. Total Time in Assigned A/C at this Station   52:50
                                                      _____

SECOND AND THIRD PHASE

                   AAF, Dyersburg, Tenn.   29 June 1944
_____ _____ _____
  Date Assigned   Station   Date Transferred to
                                                     Processing Station

1. Number of Air-to-Ground Malfunction   3
                                                     _____

2. Number of Air-to-Air Tow Missions above 20,000 feet   2
                                                     _____

3. Number of Rounds Fired above 20,000 feet   200
                                                     _____

4. Number of An Gun Camera Missions (Fighter)
                                                     _____

5. Feet of Film Used in Camera Missons
                                                     _____

6. Air-to-Air Score on 4 ft. X 20 ft. Target
                                                     _____

7. Total Time over 20,000 feet   36:05
                                                     _____

8. Total Time in Assigned A/C at this Station   84:55
                                                     _____

Pertinent remarks by the instructor of this crew member will be note on back.

SECOND AIR FORCE
GUNNERS FLYING TRAINING REPORT

Lamp, Glenn L.   Pfc.Cpl   15174303   4805
| Name | Rank | ASN | Crew Number |

14, April 1944   18th W SLC Utah
| Date Crew Activated | Group | Squadron | Station |

12:55   F.G. 44
Total Flying Time Prior to First Phase   Previous Schools Attended — Dates

FIRST PHASE

21, April 1944   AAF, Dyersburg, Tenn.
| Date Assigned | Station | Date Transferred to Second Phase |

1. Number Air-to-Ground Malfunction Missions	3
2. Number Times Operated Ball Turret	1
3. Number Times Operated Upper Turret	2
4. Proficient Checks Completed	yes
5. Total Time in Assigned A/C at this Station	52:50

SECOND AND THIRD PHASE

AAF, Dyersburg, Tenn.   29, June 1944
| Date Assigned | Station | Date Transferred to Processing Station |

1. Number of Air-to-Ground Malfunction	3
2. Number of Air-to-Air Tow Missions above 20,000 feet	2
3. Number of Rounds Fired above 20,000 feet	200
4. Number of An Gun Camera Missions (Fighter)	
5. Feet of Film Used in Camera Missons	
6. Air-to-Air Score on 4 ft. X 20 ft. Target	
7. Total Time over 20,000 feet	86:05
8. Total Time in Assigned A/C at this Station	84:55

Pertinent remarks by the instructor of this crew member will be note on back.

2ND AIR FORCE FORM
A-303 E (9-1-43)

SECOND AIR FORCE
GUNNERS FLYING TRAINING REPORT

Phillips, David A.   ~~Pvt~~ Cpl.   31399137   4805
_____   _____   _____   _____
Name   Rank   ASN   Crew Number

14, April 1944   18th RW SLC Utah
_____   _____   _____   _____
Date Crew   Group   Squadron   Station
Activated

20:05   A.G. 3/44
_____   _____
Total Flying Time   Previous Schools Attended — Dates
Prior to First Phase

FIRST PHASE

21, April 1944   AA", Dyersburg, Tenn.
_____   _____   _____
Date Assigned   Station   Date Transferred
                                                  to Second Phase

1. Number Air-to-Ground Malfunction Missions   3   .

2. Number Times Operated Ball Turret   20

3. Number Times Operated Upper Turret   4

4   Proficient Checks Completed
                                                         yes

5. Total Time in Assigned A/C at this Station   52:50

SECOND AND THIRD PHASE

                   AAF, Dyersburg, Tenn.   ~~29 June 1944~~
_____   _____   _____
Date Assigned·   Station   Date Transferred to
                                                  Processing Station

1. Number of Air-to-Ground Malfunction   3

2. Number of Air-to-Air Tow Missions above 20,000 feet   2

3. Number of Rounds Fired above 20,000 feet   200

4. Number of An Gun Camera Missions (Fighter)   /

5. Feet of Film Used in Camera Missons

6. Air-to-Air Score on 4 ft. X 20 ft. Target

7. Total Time over 20,000 feet   36:05

8. Total Time in Assigned A/C at this Station   84:55

Pertinent remarks by the instructor of this crew member will be note on back.

75

SECOND AIR FORCE
GUNNERS FLYING TRAINING REPORT

Whitaker, Robert W.	Cpl.	35697441	4805
Name	Rank	ASN	Crew Number

14, April 1944		18th RW	SLC Utah
Date Crew Activated	Group	Squadron	Station

20:20	F.G. 44	
Total Flying Time Prior to First Phase	Previous Schools Attended — Dates	

FIRST PHASE

21, April 1944	AAF. Dyersburg, Tenn.	
Date Assigned	Station	Date Transferred to Second Phase

1. Number Air-to-Ground Malfunction Missions — 3

2. Number Times Operated Ball Turret — 1

3. Number Times Operated Upper Turret — 3

4. Proficient Checks Completed — yes

5. Total Time in Assigned A/C at this Station — 52:50

SECOND AND THIRD PHASE

	AAF, Dyersburg, Tenn.	29, June 1944
Date Assigned	Station	Date Transferred to Processing Station

1. Number of Air-to-Ground Malfunction — 3

2. Number of Air-to-Air Tow Missions above 20,000 feet — 2

3. Number of Rounds Fired above 20,000 feet — 200

4. Number of An Gun Camera Missions (Fighter) —

5. Feet of Film Used in Camera Missons —

6. Air-to-Air Score on 4 ft. X 20 ft. Target —

7. Total Time over 20,000 feet — 36:05

8. Total Time in Assigned A/C at this Station — 84:55

Pertinent remarks by the instructor of this crew member will be note on back.

Bob Whitaker
Aerial Gunner
1944

Bob Whitaker
joins Army 1943

Rudy Staszko
Evade & Escape I.D.
photo 1944
England

Rudy Staszko gets Wings

KEARNEY ARMY AIR BASE

Photos courtesy of Kearney Public Library

HEADQUARTERS 271ST STAGING BASE
KEARNEY ARMY AIR FIELD
KEARNEY, NEBRASKA

370.5-1039 (198-51)   7 July 1944

SUBJECT: Movement Orders, Heavy Bombardment Crew Number FP-900-BA-33,
          To Overseas Destination.

TO: P   2nd Lt   (1024)   EDWARD C CARR   01080093
       CP 2nd Lt   (1022)   ELLIS E RICHARD   0714568
       N   2nd Lt   (1034)   EUGENE L NELSON   0723149
       B   2nd Lt   (1035)   HUGH W TREADWELL   0708027
       E   Sgt   (748)   Rudolph S Staszko   37469124
       R   Sgt   (757)   Albert D Hines   35608948
       AG Cpl   (612)   Glenn L Lamp   15174303
       CG Cpl   (611)   David A Phillips   31399137
       CG Cpl   (611)   William J Collins   33600428
       CG Cpl   (611)   Robert W Whitaker   35697441

1. You are assigned to Shipment FP-900-BA, as crew No. FP-900-BA-33,
and to B-17 airplane number 43-38038, on aircraft project number 90795-R.
You are equipped in accordance with the provisions of the movement order.

2. You are relieved from atchd unasgnd 271st AAF Base Unit (SB), this
station, and WP via mil acft and/or rail to Grenier Field, Manchester, New
Hampshire, or such other Air Port of Embarkation as the CG, ATC, may direct,
thence to the overseas destination of Shipment FP-900-BA. Upon arrival at
the Air Port of Embarkation, control of the above personnel is relinquished
to the CG, ATC.

3. This is a PERMANENT change of station. You will not be accompanied
by dependents; neither will you be joined by dependents enroute to, nor at
the Air Port of Embarkation. You will not discuss this movement except as may be
necessary in the transaction of OFFICIAL business. You will not file safe arrival
telegrams with commercial agencies while enroute and at domestic or oversea
destinations.

4. You will use APO 16305-BA (followed by the numeral ending of your
shipment crew number, underlined in paragraph 1 above), c/o Postmaster, New York,
New York. Upon arrival at final overseas destination, you will use the mailing
address of the troops at that place. Advise your friends and relatives of your
permanent APO by forwarding a completed V-Mail WD AGO Form 971; also notify the
postal officer of the theater by forwarding a completed WD AGO Form 204.

5. a. In lieu of subsistence, a flat per diem of seven dollars ($7.00)
is authorized for officers and flight officers for travel, and for periods of
temporary duty enroute to final destination, when necessary, in accordance with
existing law and regulations. Payment of mileage is not authorized. Per diem
will be suspended for such times as the individual is billeted and subsisted, as
outlined in W.D. Memo W35-2-42, dated 30 September 1942.

    b. In lieu of subsistence, a flat per diem of seven dollars ($7.00)
is authorized for enlisted men for travel, and for periods of temporary duty
enroute to final destination, in accordance with existing law and regulations, if
travel is performed by air. For travel by rail and for periods of delay enroute
to final destination, monetary allowance, in lieu of rations and quarters is prescribed in accordance with AR 35-4520.

198-61   OVERSEAS ENVELOPE

271ST AAF BASE UNIT (S.B.)
KEARNEY ARMY AIR FIELD
Kearney, Nebraska

SUBJECT: Records of Combat Crew No. **FP-900-BA-33**
Group, Shipment No. **FP-900-BA**

DATE **7 July** 19 **44**
Prov

TO   : Personnel Officer, Final Destination.

    1. In the OVERSEAS ENVELOPE which contains this letter and check list will be found the personnel records of subject heavy bombardment combat crews. It is requested that the contents of this envelope be distributed among the sections of your headquarters that are concerned.

    2. Contents of this envelope are as follows:

Quantity	ITEM	21 Wg Check	ATC Check
10	WDAGO Form 302 (M/R Locator Card)	RET	
4	WDAGO Form 66-2 (O's Qualification Record)	RET	
6	WDAGO Form 20 (EM's Qualification Card)	RET	
6	WDAGO Form 24 (Service Record), with duplicate copies authorizations for allotments.	RET	
***	WDAGO Form 971 (V-Mail Change of Address)	RET	
*	Statement of Service for Longevity (1 per officer to whom applicable)	RET	
4	Active Duty Orders (1 per officer)	RET	
x	Copies of Promotion Orders (if applicable)		
4	Copies of orders bestowing aero ratings (1 each officer)	RET	
20	Copies Orders Bestowing Flying Status (2 each)	RET	
8	Copies of orders assigning personnel to 21st Wing Station (2 for each officer)	RET	
10	Copies Travel Orders Cut by Staging Area (1 each)	RET	
10	Copies Travel Orders Cut by POAE (1 each)	X	
100	Extract Copies Orders Cut by POAE (10 each)	X	
10	AAF Form 28A (Phys. Fitness Test and Record)	RET	
10	Duplicate WD MD Form 81 (Immunization Register)	Qhe	
x	WD MD Form 78 (If Applicable)		
6	WD MD Form 79 (Dental Iden. Record) (1 per EM)	Qhe	
10	Form 21-S-17-1 (AC Supply, O and EM) (1 each)	Qh	
	(attached to Form 21-S-17-1)		
10	Form 21-S-17-2 (General Supply, O & EM) (1ea.)		
6	WDAGO Form 32 (EM's Ind. Clo. & Equipt.) (attached to Form 21-S-17-2 for each EM)		
1	Form 21-S-17-5 (Bombardier's Kit)		
1	Form 21-S-17-6 (Navigator's Kit)	Ma	
1	Form 21-S-17-7 (Ord. Equip., Crewmen Only)	EJH	
1	Form 21-S-17-8 (Ord. Equip., Non-Crewmen)		
x	Form 21-S-17-9 (AC Supply, Non-Crewmen) (if applicable)		
1x	Form 21-S-17-10 (AC Supply, Non-Flying Mechanics) (if applicable)		
10	AAF Form 5 (Individual Flight Record)	RB	
11	2AF Combat Crew Training Report Forms	RB	
1	AAF Form 12B (Bombing Records)	RB	
1	Personnel Check List (per crew) (see Form 1, annexed to PORC, WD, dated 1 April 1944)	RET	
1	Letter of Transmittal of Contents of This Envelope	RET	

    * Note: Quantity depends upon number of officers entitled to longevity.
  *** Note: Quantities vary according to number of Forms 971 desired by indi-

80

2nd Lt. Edward C. Carr   198-51   38038
CREW COMMANDER   CREW NUMBER   AIRPLANE SERIAL NO.

AUTHORIZED COLUMN IS EXACT FOR ALL THEATHERS AMENDED FOR SHIPMENT NO.

FP-900-BA-33

ORDNANCE EQUIPMENT NOMENCLATURE	AUT	ON HAND	ISS	SERIAL LOT NO	SIGNATURE	SHORT	POE ACTION
OFFICERS							
PISTOLS,auto,cal..45 comp w/holster & 2 extra clips	1	0	1	1544337	ELC		
BINOCULARS,M 21 complete	1	0	1	88-B-320			
CART.ball,cal..45 total rd 200	200	0	200	S24991			
POCKET,mag.D.webM1923(QM)	1	0	1				
PISTOL,auto,cal..45 comp w/holster & 2 extra clips	1	0	1	1544323	GCR		
POCKET,mag.D.webM1923(QM)	1	0	1				
PISTOL,auto,cal..45 comp w/holster & 2 extra clips	1	0	1	1544340	HWT		
BINOCULARS,M 21 complete	1	0	1	88-B-320			
POCKET,mag.D.webM1923(QM)	1	0	1				
PISTOL,auto,cal..45 comp w/holster & 2 extra clips	1	0	1	1544327	ELn		
POCKET,mag.D.webM1923(QM)	1	0	1				
ENLISTED MEN							
PISTOL,auto,cal..45 comp w/holster & 2 extra clips	1	0	1	1544333	IADH		
POCKET,mag.D.webM1923(QM)	1	0	1				
PISTOL,auto,cal..45 comp w/holster & 2 extra clips	1	0	1	1544315	QSS		
POCKET,mag.D.webM1923(QM)	1	0	1				
PISTOL,auto,cal..45 comp w/holster & 2 extra clips	1	0	1	1544319	GLS		
POCKET,mag.D.webM1923(QM)	1	0	1				
PISTOL,auto,cal..45 comp w/holster & 2 extra clips	1	0	1	1544338	HJC		
POCKET,mag.D.webM1923(QM)	1	0	1				
PISTOL,auto,cal..45 comp w/holster & 2 extra clips	1	0	1	1544348	RDuW.		
POCKET,mag.D.webM1923(QM)	1	0	1				
PISTOL,auto,cal..45 comp w/holster & 2 extra clips	1	0	1	1544335	DAP		
POCKET,mag.D.webM1923(QM)	1	0	1				
CLEANING & PRESERVING MAT							
ROD,cleaning,cal..45M4	2	0	2				
BRUSH,cleaning,brass,	2	0	2				
SCREWDRIVER,pistol,cal45	2	0	2				
OILER,cir.flat,brass	1	0	1				
OIL.lub.2-27d or AXS-777	1	0	1				
PATCHES,cut canton flanel	100	0	100				
INSTRUCTIONS,Maint. pistol cal..45	10	0	10				

I hereby acknowledge receipt of all articles in the "Issued" column and
certify that none of this equipment has previously been issued for this
crew,and that the articles listed in the "ON HAND" column are in possession
of the crew.

Edward C Carr 2d Lt AC
PILOTS SIGNATURE

CERTIFICATE OF MEDICAL FITNESS

Location **AAF, Kearney, Nebraska**   Date   **7 July 1944**

STATION	RANK & NAME		ASN	IMMUNI-ZATION	DENTAL STATUS
PILOT	Carr, Edward C.	2nd Lt	0-1080093	Complete	IV
CO-PILOT	Richard, Ellis E.	2nd Lt	0-714568	Complete	IV
NAVIGATOR	Nelson, Eugene L.	2nd Lt	0-723149	Complete	IV
BOMBARDIER	Treadwell, Hugh W.	2nd Lt	0-708027	Complete	IV
RADIO OP	Staszko, Rudolph S.	Sgt	37469124	Complete	IV
ENGINEER	Hines, Albert D.	Sgt	35608948	Complete	IV
ASS'T ENG	Lemp, Glenn L.	Cpl	15174303	Complete	IV
ASS'T R/OP	Phillips, David A.	Cpl	31399137	Complete	IV
GUNNER	Collins, William J.	Cpl	33600428	Complete	IV
GUNNER	Whitaker, Robert W.	Cpl	35697441	Complete	IV
PASSENGER					

1. I have examined the above members of Heavy Bombardment Crew No._____ on _____**7 July** 19.**44**, and have found them physically qualified for foreign duty.

2. I certify that the above men have been blood grouped and have been completely immunized against typhoid, smallpox, tetanus, typhus, cholera and yellow fever except as noted.

3. I certify that the above men are dentally Class IV except as noted.

Charles P. Catalano
Charles P Catalano Captain MC
Processing Surgeon

Note:
(Use word Complete for immunization or state those required. Show Class I, II, ID, or IV for dental)

21-M-1 (21 August 1943)   Certificate of Medical Fitness

REQUISITION AND SHIPPING TICKET (DOMESTIC)

| DATE PREPARED: | PREPARED BY: gma | BASIS FOR REQUISITION: | DATE OF ACTION: 7-8-44 | CLASS: 05-A | AUTHORITY OR REQUISITION NO. AAF Regulations 65-27 and 15-121 | SHIPPING OFFICER'S VOUCHER NO. 15-44 |

SHIPPED FROM: AAF-333 SO

SHIPPED TO: AAF 43-38038 ... SHIPMENT # FP-900-DA-33 Kearney, Nebraska

ACCOUNTABILITY:

SHIP VIA: Personal Delivery ROUTING:

ITEM	ORDERED	STOCK RECORD ACTION		WAREHOUSE ACTION		HDQTRS. ACTION	UNIT OF ISSUE	STOCK NUMBER	NOMENCLATURE
		CODE	CHANGED TO	SHIPPED	CHANGED TO	ITEM TALLY			
1	3			3			ea.	6200479800	WATCH-Navigation, Type A-11

NOTHING FOLLOWS

We certify that the article listed hereon has not previously been issued to us.

Edward C. Carr

EDWARD C. CARR, 2d Lt., O1080093, Pilot

Ellis E. Richard

ELLIS E. RICHARD, 2d Lt., 0714568, Co-Pilot

Albert D. Hines

ALBERT D. HINES, Sgt., 35608948, ROG

I certify that I have this date issued 1 ea. of the item listed hereon to each one of the persons who accomplished the foregoing certificate, and the above item has been entered on AAF Form 121, Individual Issue Record, which has been delivered to each one of the above-named individuals.

WAYNE D. DEY, 2nd Lt., AC
Ass't AAF-333 SO

| CODE FOR ACTION TAKEN | V-BEING SHIPPED | X-EXTRACTED | B-BACK ORDERED | O-CANCELLED | E-ADDITIONAL INFORMATION REQUIRED |

REQUISITION AND SHIPPING TICKET (DOMESTIC)

| DATE PREPARED: | PREPARED BY: | BASIS FOR REQUISITION: | DATE OF ACTION: 7-8-44 | CLASS: 13 | AUTHORITY OR REQUISITION NO. 65-23 and 15-121 | SHIPPING OFFICER'S VOUCHER NO. 901-45 |

SHIPPED FROM:

SHIPPED TO: SHIP # 43-38038 CREW# FP-900-DA-33 KEARNEY, NEB.

ITEM	ORDERED						UNIT OF ISSUE	STOCK NUMBER	NOMENCLATURE
1							EA	3300541700	JACKET FLYING, WINTER TYPE B-11 SIZE 36
2			8				EA	3300541705	JACKET FLYING WINTER, TYPE B-11 SIZE 38
3							EA	3300541710	JACKET FLYING WINTER, TYPE B-11 SIZE 40
4			2				EA	3300541715	JACKET FLYING WINTER, TYPE B-11 SIZE 42
5							EA	3300541720	JACKET FLYING WINTER, TYPE B-11 SIZE 44
6							PR	3300933750	TROUSERS WINTER FLYING TYPE A-10A SIZE 36
7			8				PR	3300933855	TROUSERS WINTER FLYING TYPE A-10A SIZE 38
8							PR	3300933860	TROUSERS WINTER FLYING TYPE A-10A SIZE 40
9			2				PR	3300933865	TROUSERS WINTER FLYING TYPE A-10A SIZE 42
10							PR	3300933870	TROUSERS WINTER FLYING TYPE A-10A SIZE 44

WE CERTIFY THAT THE ARTICLES LISTED HEREON HAVE NOT PREVIOUSLY BEEN ISSUED TO US.

PILOT: *Edward C. Carr*   RADIO: *Albert D. Hines*

CO-PILOT: *Ellis E. Richard*   AG: *Glenn L. Lamp*

NAVIGATOR: *Eugene F. Nelson*   CG: *William J. Collins*

BOMBARDIER: *Hugh W. Treadwell*   CG: *David A. Phillips*

ENGINEER: *R S Stosylko*   CG: *Robert W. Whitaker*

| CODE FOR ACTION TAKEN | V-BEING SHIPPED | X-EXTRACTED | B-BACK ORDERED | O-CANCELLED | E-ADDITIONAL INFORMATION REQUIRED |

GRENIER FIELD
MANCHESTER, N. H.
STA. 16, NAV, ATC

(OPERATIONS ORDERS)

No..........118)

E X T R A C T

SECRET
AUTH: CO STA. 16
7-8-44

8 July 1944

** ** ** **

10. The following named crews WP by air in the aircraft as indicated below at the proper time from Grenier Field, Manchester, New Hampshire, via North Atlantic Route, to the European Theatre of Operations, London, England, reporting upon arrival thereat to the Commander, 8th Air Force Service Command, Air Transport Command Terminals of Arrival, British Isles, for further assignment and duty with the 8th Air Force.

Shipment No. FP- -BA-18, Project No. 90795-R, APO No. 16305-BA-18
B-17G   Crew No. FP- -BA-18   #43-38022

2nd Lt.	JACKSON, RAYMOND F.	0819821	(P)
2nd Lt.	SHERRILL, THEODORE I.	0705148	(CP)
2nd Lt.	FRANKE, JOHN H., JR.	0718275	(N)
2nd Lt.	PLEVAK, EDWARD C.	0708099	(B)
Pvt.	Nelson, Laverne W.	36737327	(E)
Sgt.	Michael, George R.	15328232	(R)
Pvt.	Harcq, Benjamin W., Jr.	16080380	(AG)
Pvt.	Krewer, Charles R.	36732876	(CG)
Cpl.	Ballard, Bennie L.	38470348	(CG)
Pvt.	Rogers, Willie	14137225	(CG)

Shipment No. FP- -BA-16, Project No. 90795-R, APO No. 16305-BA-16
B-17G   Crew No. FP- -BA-16   #43-38018

2nd Lt.	FISHER, WILLIAM S.	0819781	(P)
2nd Lt.	BONNELL, WILLIAM C., JR.	0714628	(CP)
2nd Lt.	EKBLOM, ROBERT, JR.	0723328	(N)
2nd Lt.	PHIPPS, RUPERT L.	0707437	(B)
Sgt.	Peterson, David M.	36818325	(E)
Cpl.	Ratica, Herman J.	13086759	(R)
Pfc.	Gillespie, Stanley P.	37578695	(AG)
Pfc.	Levonian, Ernest L.	39282712	(CG)
Pfc.	Brantley, Cecil B.	34854382	(CG)
Pfc.	Lawson, Buford B.	34884913	(CG)

Shipment No. FP- -BA-33, Project No. 90795-R, APO No. 16305-BA-33
B-17G   Crew No. FP- -BA-33   #43-38038

2nd Lt.	CARR, EDWARD C.	01080093	(P)
2nd Lt.	RICHARD, ELLIS E.	0714568	(CP)
2nd Lt.	NELSON, EUGENE L.	0723149	(N)
2nd Lt.	TREADWELL, HUGH W.	0708027	(B)
Sgt.	Staszko, Rudolph S.	37469124	(E)
Sgt.	Hines, Albert D.	35608948	(R)
Cpl.	Lamp, Glenn L.	15174303	(AG)
Cpl.	Phillips, David A.	31399137	(CG)
Cpl.	Collins, William J.	33600428	(CG)
Cpl.	Whitaker, Robert W.	35697441	(CG)

-1-

SECRET

EXTRACT 10, Operations Orders No. 118, Sta. 16, NW, ATC, Grenier Field,
Manchester, N.H.   8 July 1944   P2

Shipment No. FB- -CJ-196, Project No. 92766-R; APO.No. 16209-CJ-196
B-17G   Crew No. FB- -CJ-196   #43-37960

2nd Lt.	CHADWICK, JAMES W.	0764608	(P)
2nd Lt.	GRANTHAM, EDGAR H.	0824132	(CP)
2nd Lt.	WHITE, LESLIE C.	0718473	(N)
2nd Lt.	VEHERYKE, ROBERT M.	0769322	(B)
Cpl.	Brown, Virgil D.	36074292	(E)
Cpl.	Mulvey, Lawrence V.	13070555	(R)
Cpl.	Atkins, Byron L.	35146697	(AG)
Cpl.	Schoonover, Henry K.	35760646	(CG)
Cpl.	Merfeld, Louis L.	37680091	(CG)
Cpl.	Klumpp, Kenneth B.	36706226	(CG)

This is a PERMANENT change of station.
Except as may be necessary in the transaction of official business,
individuals are prohibited from discussing their oversea destination even by
shipment number. They will not file safe arrival telegrams with
commercial agencies while enroute and at domestic or oversea destinations.
In lieu of subsistence a flat per diem of seven dollars ($7.00) is
authorized for travel and for periods of temporary duty enroute to final
destination, when necessary for officers and flight officers, in accordance
with existing law and regulations. Payment of mileage is not authorized.
Such times as the individual is billeted and subsisted, as outlined in WD
Memorandum W-35-2-42, 30 Sept. 1942, his per diem will be suspended.
A flat per diem of seven dollars ($7.00) is authorized for enlisted men
for travel and for periods of temporary duty enroute to final destination, in
accordance with existing law and regulations, if travel is performed by air.
For travel by rail and for periods of delay enroute to final destination,
monetary allowance in lieu of rations and quarters is prescribed in accordance
with AR-35-4520.
TDN. 501-31 P 431-01-02-03-04-05-07-08 212/50425.
From time of departure from the continental United States until arrival
at permanent overseas station, payment of per diem is authorized for a maximum
of forty-five (45) days.
The information contained in Paragraphs 26 and 27 of "Preparation for
Oversea Movement for AAF Replacement Combat Crews, dtd 1 April 1944, consti-
tutes an integral part of this order.
AUTH: Ltr fr CG, AAF to CG, ATC, Sub: "Assignment and Reassignment of
Military Personnel of the AAF", 12/1/42 and 1st Ind fr CG, ATC, to CG, NAW,
12/10/42 and AR 55-120 Par. 3b(2) 1943; NAW, ATC, by 1st Ind dtd 15 April 44
to Ltr CG, ATC, dtd 7 Feb. 1944.
**   **   **   **

By order of Col. MOORE

J. E. SANDOW
Lt. Col., AC
Aircraft Operations Officer

OFFICIAL: *Kenneth Libby*
KENNETH LIBBY
W.O. (jg) USA
Ass't Aircraft Operations Officer.
-2-

SHIPPING TICKET

PREPARED BY .... SHIPPING OFFICER'S VOUCHER NO. ....

DATE 7-8-44   SHIPPING ORDER: CLASS .... NO. ....   PAGE ....

TRANSIENT SUPPLY OFFICER
CONSIGNOR CRESIER FIELD, MANCHESTER, N. H.

CONSIGNEE EDWARD C. CARR, 2nd Lt., AC, PILOT

DATE SHIPPED

ACCOUNTABILITY SHIP # 43-38038   GROUP # FP-900-BA-33

SHIP BY   SELECTED BY

AUTH. OR REG. NO. ....   INSPECTED BY   PACKED BY

B/L NO. ....   ROUTING

STOCK LOCATION	ITEM	QUANTITY ORDERED	CHANGED TO	UNIT	PART NO.	NAME	UNIT COST	TOTAL COST
	1.			pr.		Glasses, sun, flying ////////(end)///////		

We certify that the articles listed hereon have not
previously been issued to us.

[signatures]
Edward C. Carr   Albert P. Hince
Ellis E. Richert   Glenn L. Lamp
Eugene L. Nelson   William J. Collins
Hugh M. Treadwell   David A. Phillips
R. S. Staszko   Robert W. Whitaker

I certify that I have this date issued to
listed hereon to the person who accomplished the foregoing certificate, and the above listed items have been
entered on AAF Form 101, Individual Issue Record, which
has been delivered to the above-named individual.

(Signature) Edward M. Gladue
EDWARD M. GLADUE
1st Lt., AC
Transient Supply Officer

THIS COPY TO ....   RECEIVED ....   DATE ....

NAME AND RANK   RECEIVING OFFICER'S VOUCHER NO. ....

SIGNATURE   POSTED TO STOCK RECORD BY ....

LABRADOR LOU says LUCK TO YOU

While on this Base:
Help us <u>avoid</u> <u>risk</u> <u>of</u> <u>fire</u>
Remain on immediate Base area
(Obtain pass before leaving it)

Use our Recreation Hall for:
Reading, Bowling, Playing Basketball,
Ping-pong, Pool

Visit our Theatre, Athletic field, and
Chaplains' Offices.

We trust your stay here will be pleasant.

WELCOME TRANSIENT PERSONNEL

When leaving your airplane:
<u>Take</u> complete uniform & toilet articles
<u>Leave</u> coveralls, arms & cameras

Base personnel are required to:
Wear regulation uniforms & insignia
Observe military courtesy
Keep quarters clean & orderly

Your cooperation will help.

We are your hosts

Welcome to Labrador's
Wonderland

If you need a car to go to your airplane,
transportation is available at operations bldg.

If you sleep late, our PX coffee shop opens at
1200 GMT, except Saturday

There are good lounges for your comfort and
pleasure in the Briefing Building--
one for Enlisted Men; one for Officers

AMERICAN RED CROSS

"July 12, 1944
Somewhere in Iceland"

Dear Mother,

I don't imagine that you expected a letter from us this way. Well don't be too surprised the next one will probably be from some place else. Have not been here long and will be glad to get out of here for it is quite a desolate place.

Can't complain though I have finally reached a cool climate. After Tenn. & Nebraska this is O.K. and I feel a lot better.

This place has me plenty confused as to time of day. During this time of the year it is light almost 24 hours a day. Seems odd to be going to bed at 11 or 12 o'clock when it is as light as day out.

I wrote Mike from Nebraska but was not sure of his address. Will you give me his and Dougs.

Still have the same crew that I started with in Dyersburg and they have turned out swell. Hope they don't break us up because I would not want to loose any one of them.

Give me all the dope in Waco and on how the coach likes his new station. Lots of love

Ed

War Department   WAR DEPARTMENT
A.A.F. Form No. 99   Army Air Forces
Revised May 14, 1942   xDebit xCredit

MEMORANDUM RECEIPT

No. _____

Station _56 8 - Valley. Wales_   Date _15-7-44_

Issuing _Ball - Edward C - 2d Lt_

Issued to Detachment B, Supply Section BAD No. 1

Quantity	Unit	Part No.	Article
1		B17 G	Type and contents listed on AC Form 263 and 263A
			A/C Serial No. _43- 3 8 0 3 8_
			Flight Order No. _FP- BA-33_
			Project No. _907 95 - R_
			Confidential Equipment Installed on this A/C
			Radio _Yes_
			Bombsight _Yes_

I acknowledge receipt of the above listed Army Air Forces
Property:

xStrike Out Words not Applicable   _Robert B Helfrich_
ROBERT B. HELFRICH,
Capt, AC, Comdg.

Receipt for delivery of one B–17 G to Army Air Force Detachment,
Valley Wales

1. IF QUARTERS OR RATIONS WERE FURNISHED - PER DIEM CAN NOT BE CLAIMED.
2. EACH OFFICER IS RESPONSIBLE FOR THE FACTS STATED HEREON.

PER DIEM ITINERARY SHEET

NAME Edward C. Carr RANK 2nd Lt. ASN O-1080293

PER DIEM CLAIMED FROM 7 July 1944 to 16 July 1944

PREVIOUS PAYMENTS OF PER DIEM TO INCL None 19

BY AT

TRAVEL BY Air (METHOD OF CONVEYANCE).

	STATION	TIME	DATE
DEPARTED	Kearney, Neb.	0200	8 July 44
ARRIVED	Grenier Fld., N.H.	1300	8 July 44
DELAY:			
DEPARTED	Grenier Fld., N.H.	0800	10 July 44
ARRIVED	Goose Bay, Lab.	1530	10 July 44
DELAY:	1 Day Waiting orders		
DEPARTED	Goose Bay, Lab.	0800	11 July 44
ARRIVED	Meeks Fld., Iceland	1600	11 July 14
DELAY:	4 days Weather		
DEPARTED	Meeks Fld. Iceland	0800	15 July 44
ARRIVED	Valley, Wales	1530	15 July 44
DELAY:			
DEPARTED	Valley, Wales	1500	16 July 44
ARRIVED	Stone	2000	16 July 44
DELAY:			
DEPARTED			
ARRIVED			
DELAY:			
DEPARTED			
ARRIVED			
DELAY:			
DEPARTED			
ARRIVED			
DELAY:			
DEPARTED			
ARRIVED			
DELAY:			
DEPARTED			
ARRIVED			
DELAY:			

(SIGNED) Edward C. Carr
2nd Lt. A.C.

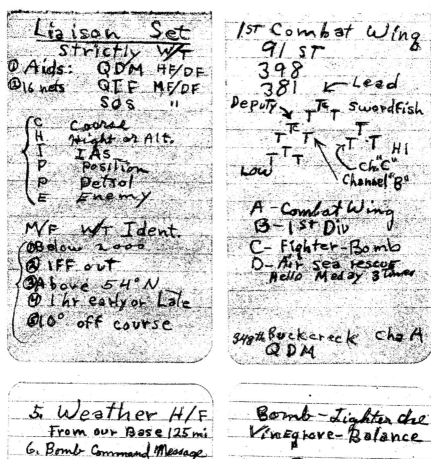

Liaison Set
Strictly W/T

① Aids: QDM HF/DF
② 16 nets QTF MF/DF
        SOS "

{
- C Coorse
- H Hight or Alt.
- I IAS
- P Position
- P Petrol
- E Enemy
}

MF W/T Ident.
① Below 2000
② IFF out
③ Above 54° N
④ 1 hr early or Late
⑤ 10° off course

1st Combat Wing
  91 ST
  398
  381 ← Lead
Deputy ↘ ↑ T↑ swordfish
      T⁻ᵀC T
     T⁻ᵀ   T   T·T Hi
Low J⁻ᵀ T   ↰ Ch."C"
          Channel"B"

A – Combat Wing
B – 1st Div
C – Fighter-Bomb
D – Air sea rescue
  Hello Meday 3 Tower

348th Buckcreek cha A
  QDM

---

5. Weather H/F
  From our Base 125 mi
6. Bomb Command Message
  H/F
Command Set
10 mile range
① #1 – 6440 KCS
  #2 – 5210 KCS
Aids Control Tower
  code name
② Darky
    OCCULT – one
letter in white
③ Ballon Barrage
Squeakers

Bomb – Lighter die
Vinegrove – Balance

IFF – Only in
distress

1st Div Buncher
1040 kc 8P8

Ed Carr's class notes
Replacement Center, Bovingdon, England
July 1944

Take Off
Group leader (white)
Tail high on take off
Position of turbo
ampliphiers

V H F

A. Plane to Plane
B. Air To Division
C. US & RAF fighters
D. Emergency (SOS)
75 - 125 miles range

IFF

Radio Compass

CW Position
14 M/F Fixed Beacons
    225 miles
Jamming
Meaconing 7A7
series of dots through
call sign
4 nulls when
meaconed
16 Splasher 7A7
off Day light 300 miles
4 min. Buncher 8A8
One per. wing 45 miles
during missions
  U.S. beacons
   Forming & Let Down

H F/D F
   3000 - 7000 KC
1. QDM
2. QTF
3. Permission S13A
4. Diversion
5. Recall
6. Area weather
7. " field condition
8. W/T Link To B/S

{ Bassingbourne
{ RGT - 3570
{ Combat Wing

B/s NG 8 4525 kc
1. QDM
2. Cir SBA
3. Diversion
4. Recall
5. Local weather
6.   " field condition
7. Gen. air to ground
   R/T Control tower
{
1. 5065 KC
2. 6440 KC
Clydesdale
10 - 15 miles

Divisional Freq
6635 - 7 MT
Brampton

Flying Control

Only left hand
Traffic at night

White X's or Yellow
flags (red Lights at night)
means an obstruction

Q - signals

QDM- Bearing you To Sta.
QFE- Bar. Pres not
    reduced To sea level
QFF- Bar. Pres. sea level
QUB- Weather report
QDR- Bearing Sta To You
QDY- Ballon barrage on QDM
QKJ- May I approach
using beam approach
        Installation

QKF- May I land
using beam approach
    Installation
QTE(MF/DF) What
is my true bearing
from you
QTF (MF/DF) Will
you give me a
fix
  Non operational

Darky

Hello Darky - Hello Darky
Hello Darky this is
Squadron name + ship Letter
3 times
Q are you receiving me
Q " " " " "
(over)
Mayday = SOS
   3 times

Ditching Proc.

Emergency
Radio

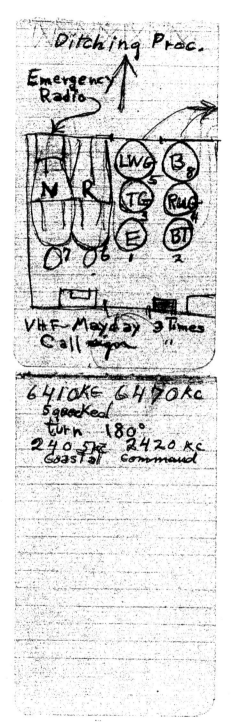

VHF- Mayday 3 Times
   Call sign "

6410KC 6470kc
Squeaked
turn 180°
2405kc 2420 kc
Coastal command

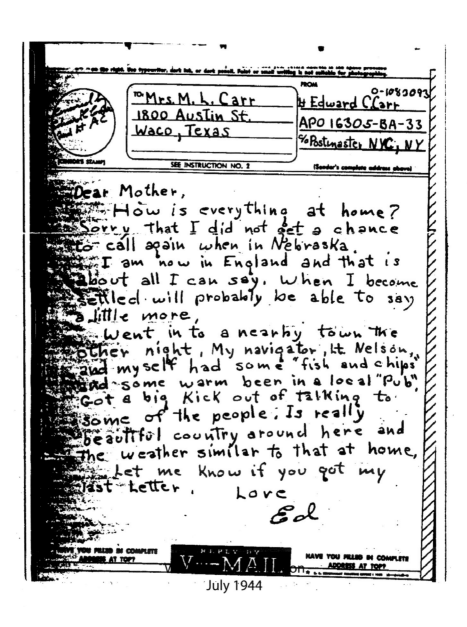

TO: **Mrs. M. L. Carr**
1800 Austin St.
Waco, Texas

FROM: # Edward C Carr   O-1083093
APO 16305-BA-33
%Postmaster, NYC, NY

SEE INSTRUCTION NO. 2   (Sender's complete address above)

Dear Mother,
How is everything at home?
Sorry that I did not get a chance
to call again when in Nebraska.
I am now in England and that is
about all I can say. When I become
settled will probably be able to say
a little more,
Went into a nearby town the
other night, My navigator, Lt. Nelson,
and myself had some "fish and chips"
and some warm been in a local "Pub".
Got a big kick out of talking to
some of the people; Is really
beautiful country around here and
the weather similar to that at home,
Let me know if you got my
last letter.   Love
                    Ed

HAVE YOU FILLED IN COMPLETE
ADDRESS AT TOP?

V---MAIL

HAVE YOU FILLED IN COMPLETE
ADDRESS AT TOP?

July 1944

CHAPTER 6

Replacements

Valley, Wales to Stone, England (Replacement Depots),

and

Bovingdon (CCRC-Combat Crew Replacement Center),

and

Snettisham (Combat Crew Gunnery School)

Stone, England, Station 594 was the home of the 14th and 16th Replacement Depots. My records show that we traveled to Stone on a Sunday, leaving Valley, Wales, about 3 p.m. and arriving about 8 p.m. on 16 July 1944. The crews referred to the Replacement Depot as the "Repple-Depple." I don't recall how long we were at Stone. Gene Nelson's diary shows we were there a week until 23 July. The enlisted men on the crew then went on to the Training Squadron at AAF Station 172. This was the Combat Crew Gunnery School at Snettisham near the Wash, that shallow sea that is the north border to East Anglia. The Wash was used extensively by the Eighth Air Force for practice bombing and gunnery training. Rudy Staszko recalls that the gunnery training consisted of ground-to-air firing of 50 caliber machine guns at a target sleeve towed by an aircraft along the shoreline. According to Rudy they tried to sever the towline with their tracers, making for very hazardous duty for the pilot of the tow plane. They all knew that the real way to learn aerial gunnery was to fire from a moving bomber at an attacking fighter.

Aside from their gunnery training at Snettisham, the crew attended Eighth Air Force familiarization classes. They received the mandatory lecture about off-base conduct when associating with the civilian population. Rudy tells of an unofficial code of conduct. He and other gunners were told by their veteran instructors that they should always take their raincoats when going off-base on pass. This was a courtesy to the British women who appreciated not getting their dresses wet on moist grass.

The commissioned officers of the crew went on from Stone to the CCRC (Combat Crew Replacement Center) near Bovingdon, a short distance northwest of London. We were assigned to the 1st Replacement and Training Squadron (B), AAF Station 112. This was to be our home for about two weeks.

Assignments from the Replacement Center to a Bomb Group were based on the crew needs of the Eighth Air Force Groups. B-17 crews went to Groups in the First or Third Divisions of the 8th, and B-24 crews went to Groups of the Second Air Division. Aside from training, the main occupation of the officers was waiting, circumstances that provided fertile ground for rumors. The rumors were mainly centered around which Bomb Group was the best or worst assignments, which had the highest combat loss ratio, which had the best or worst location. All kinds of opinions were expressed. The consensus was that an assignment to the 100th Bomb Group, known as the Bloody 100th, was equivalent to a death sentence. The merits of the other Groups were hotly debated.

While waiting for our assignment we went to classes. We were given thorough indoctrination in the Eighth Air Force way of doing things. Hourly classes covered a wide variety of subjects. Flight Control Systems were covered. Squadron, Group and Division assembly methods, formation flying, high altitude flight problems, fighter tactics, aircraft identification, ditching procedures, air-sea rescue, European geography were all classroom subjects. The radio communication systems used in the United Kingdom by the 8th Air Force were gone over in great detail. Instructors cautioned us about the use of foul language on the radio. Combat radio frequencies were monitored by women of the RAF (the WAAF's). In the excitement of combat, fliers, particularly fighter pilots, forgot themselves and uttered some four-letter words. The concern of headquarters about the sensibilities of the young women listening to the radio signals says something about the moral code of the 1940's.

The ground-to-air and air-to-ground radio communication systems devised by the British and the American Air Force had to overcome and solve some unique problems. There was a complete blackout at night. Lights of cities, towns, and roads could not be used as visual checkpoints for navigation. Frequently clouds or fog obscured the ground. In order to secure a location fix, a system called DARKY was established. England was divided into quadrants with radio receiving stations of limited range located at the intersection of quadrant lines. A plane wanting to determine location would call DARKY on the proper frequency three times: "Hello, Darky, Hello, Darky, Hello Darky." Then the caller gave the Squadron code name and plane letter three times: "This is Swordfish Charlie, this is Swordfish Charlie, this is Swordfish Charlie." Then three times: "Are you receiving me? Are you receiving me? Are you receiving me? Over." The nearest DARKY radio receiving station would be the one with the best radio reception and know that the plane was in that station's quadrant. A quadrant location fix would be relayed by radio to the plane. The fix was accurate down to a few miles.

The numerous airfields in East Anglia for bombers and fighters of the Eighth Air Force, plus many RAF fields, created a communication nightmare. To avoid interference between radio control towers of one airfield with another, the range of each station's signal was limited to a ten-mile radius. Thus if a plane could receive a radio signal from a control tower, it was within ten miles of that field. Our intrepid crew was to prove that this system was not infallible.

After we had been on combat status for several months, our Headquarters decided that flight crews should stay proficient in night flying, even though all 8th Air Force missions were daylight raids. Our turn came and we were scheduled for a night training flight over England. After completing our prescribed flight plan, I asked our navigator for a heading to our base at Ridgewell. At our ETA over Ridgewell I called on the Ridgewell frequency for landing instructions and requested that the runway landing lights be turned on. In reply we were given the runway heading and almost directly below us we saw the runway lights go on. We made a normal let down and went into a required left-hand pattern for a night landing. On final approach we turned on our landing lights. When about to touch down I realized that the concrete pattern of the runway surface looked unfamiliar. Rolling down the runway I saw, off to our right, the silhouettes of parked bombers. They were not B-17's, but Lancaster bombers of the Royal Air Force. It was too late for a touch-and-go landing. At the end of the runway we turned onto the perimeter track and we continued to taxi in order to circle back to the head of the runway on which we had just landed. I could not figure out why the runway lights of the RAF field had been turned on at the time I was talking to the Ridgewell tower. While we taxied I was still receiving the radio signal from Ridgewell. They wanted to know when we would be landing. To assist us in locating the field they said they would fire a red-green flare. On the horizon I saw a flare arc into the night sky. Since we were receiving the Ridgewell radio, while on the ground at an RAF airbase, I figured they could probably hear us, so I responded reporting that we had seen the flares and would be landing soon. As we taxied, an RAF jeep drove out to meet us. We stopped briefly; Rudy jumped out and advised the driver we would be on our way back to our own base. He got back in and we continued to the runway for a quick take off. After a short flight, we landed at Ridgewell. We guessed that the RAF had identified our plane and that we would catch hell on return to Ridgewell, but nothing was said to us and we volunteered no information!

Some weeks later another night training flight was scheduled. The briefing officer gave us a stern lecture about unauthorized landings at RAF bases. Because the control tower at the RAF field failed to note the serial number of a plane from our Group that had made a night landing, the plane could not be identified. The briefing officer expounded to the assembled crews on the stupidity of such a pilot and crew. With innocent expressions on our faces we nodded our assent. We knew we were never going to convince this guy that we had been misled by freak atmospheric conditions that extended the Ridgewell radio signal beyond the ten-mile limit.

One lecture at the Replacement Center covered off-base conduct. We were not to forget that we were guests and allies of the British. Things to remember: a person from Wales or Scotland is not English, but is British; queues are a way of life and a sure way to offend was to cut in front of people standing in line; rationing had impacted all facets of life; things look shabby by our standards, but that is because of the war effort; clothes are mended, not replaced; be aware of the fact that many families have lost loved ones in the war.

Because we were there only two weeks my memory of the Bovingdon Replacement Center is not very clear. I do recall that the center was near the towns of Hemel Hempstead and Watford. I wrote a V-mail letter from Bovingdon reporting that I was now in England. In the letter I wrote that Gene Nelson and I went to a nearby town, had some fish and chips and warm beer in a local pub and enjoyed talking to some of the people. That letter triggered memories of some first encounters with the British.

In the pub I recall being asked by one of the regulars if we had just come across the pond. I didn't know how to respond. Then I realized he was referring to the Atlantic Ocean, a British pond for several centuries. Walking over a stone bridge on our way to town we heard a warning beep from a bicycle approaching from our rear. A young girl coasted her bike onto the bridge. She was rotating the bike pedals backwards. Not realizing that British bikes did not use coaster brakes, I asked her why she was pedaling backwards. She replied, "Oh that's for clauss", not "class" as we would pronounce the word. Then with a friendly smile and a wave, she rode off pedaling in a normal manner.

One of my clear memories of our Bovingdon days was the sighting of a Buzz Bomb. Walking on our way to a class, several of us heard a strange putt-putt sound from the sky. We spotted the V-1 approaching from the east. It had stubby wings and a pipe-like pulse jet engine on top that pushed it to a speed exceeding most propeller-driven aircraft. At about 1,000 feet altitude it crossed on a westerly heading just north of where we stood. After it passed, the sound suddenly cut off. There was silence, then moments later a large explosion. The Buzz Bomb, along with the ballistic rocket V-2, was one of Hitler's secret weapons. The V-1 was scary because it was an inaccurate terror weapon. The one we saw at Bovingdon was probably aimed at London but overshot its target. The V-1 carried a two-thousand-pound warhead. If from the ground one heard the engine cut off, you were probably safe because it would likely glide for a time before diving to the ground. Civilians were its target, the same as the V-2. A pure ballistic rocket, faster than sound, it was never heard coming.

In the months ahead, when on leave in London, we would become acquainted with the V-2's. I remember the sound, a tremendous

"THRUMP", and knowing that another one hit some place in the city. There were no air raid warnings for the V-2 rockets, but Londoners still took to the Underground (the tube) for protection when under attack. During one of our London visits, a V-2 came down through the top of a large department store on Oxford Street killing many shoppers. Both the Royal Air Force and the Eighth Air Force made raids on the research and launching facilities of the rockets, reducing the numbers available for Hitler's terror raids.

Gene Nelson tells the story of an unauthorized excursion to Hemel Heamstead. We were not given passes to leave the base at Bovingdon, but the four of us—Gene, Ellis, Hugh and I—decided to go to Hemel Heamstead. We took a cab to town and arranged to be picked up at 11 p.m. at the town square. Of course there was a blackout and Gene said that an air raid siren signaled a night raid. We became separated. Gene recalls that he and Rich met two milkmaids in a tearoom. It was difficult in the blackout, in a strange town, to locate the square. Hugh didn't show up. Rich (Ellis) arrived at the meeting place with a girl on his arm. The cab dropped us, without Hugh, at a wooded area near our barracks. About midnight a sergeant came to the barracks looking for Lt. Carr. They had Hugh Treadwell, our bombardier, in the guardhouse. He had been picked up without a pass. Hugh was released from custody and returned to our quarters.

CHAPTER 7

The Last Leg

Replacement Center to 381st Bomb Group, Ridgewell

Special Order 217 of 4 August 1944 assigned five new crews to the 381st Bomb Group. The orders also appointed me to be the officer in charge of the crews going to AAF Station 167 at Ridgewell. We were to travel by Government Vehicle and Rail on 5 August. The enlisted men on Temporary Duty at AAF Station 172, the Combat Crew Gunnery School, would travel to the 381st on the same date. Although I was the officer in charge, I do not remember that first trip to Ridgewell. Maybe the intensity of experiences in the following days blotted out the memory of that trip. Logically we would have traveled from Bovingdon to London by rail, then from Liverpool Station northeasterly to Colchester. From there we probably transferred to the line going west up the beautiful Colne Valley, through Halstead and Sible Hedringham to Great Yeldham. There was no station at Ridgewell. We would have left the train at the Great Yeldham station and traveled to the airbase by truck.

Of the five crews assigned to the 381st on 4 August 1944, two crews on 5 August 1944 were assigned to the 533rd Bomb Squadron—Bob Gotthardt's crew and our crew. Bob and I started our careers with the 381st the same day. Months later, in the winter of 1945, we took separate paths, his leading to a tragic end. More than just a fellow pilot, Bob became a friend. We were both from the Pacific Northwest. He was from Longview, Washington; I was from Tacoma. We used to swap stories over drinks in the officers club and flew in the 533rd Squadron formations on some of the same missions. The Mission Formation Sheet for the 200th mission of the 381st BG on 9 October 1944 to Schweinfurt, Germany, shows Gotthardt's crew was in the lead of the low element; Carr's crew was in formation on his right wing and assigned to monitor Channel B, the fighter-bomber radio channel.

Bob was a natural leader and dedicated to doing his best for the Squadron. We had both been promoted to 1st Lieutenant in the fall of 1944. When he finished his 35th mission, Bob decided to volunteer for a second tour. Pilots and other crewmembers who had taken leadership positions were urged to volunteer for a second tour. Lieutenants were promoted to captain and flew only formation lead positions. Bob had just finished his last mission when he came to see me in February 1945 just before my 35th and last mission. He tried to persuade me to volunteer for a second tour. I told him that I would think about it, but I was not going to decide until my last mission was crossed off on the small calendar I kept.

After my last mission Bob and I met again. I clearly recall the circumstances of our discussion. He was facing me and sitting on a bunk next to mine in my Nissen Hut. I told him that after the 14 February mission, one of the roughest I had been on, that I had made up my mind not to volunteer for more missions. When he realized that he was going to have trouble convincing me to sign up for a second tour, Bob told me that one of his new duties was to be the Group's Awards Officer. He was an experienced writer having been, in civilian life, a reporter for the Portland Oregonian Newspaper. He then proceeded to interview me about some of my missions, particularly the last one. Bob had decided on the spot that I was to be recommended for a Distinguished Flying Cross (the DFC). He planned to write up a citation and submit it through channels to the Group Commander for approval. I suggested to Bob that he was trying to bribe me, first with a promotion to Captain and secondly with a DFC in order to get me to volunteer, against my better judgment, for another combat tour. What I should have told him was that he should not push his own luck. He had done enough in flying one combat tour. But Bob had made up his mind to stay with the Squadron for another tour. I was unable to convince him otherwise.

On the mission of 22 March 1945 to Dorsten/Feldhausen, Germany, Captain Robert Gotthardt was Command Pilot in the lead plane. His B-17 received a flak burst between the number three engine and the fuselage. The plane's location was 5134 North and 0700 East at 24,000 feet when it burst into flames and started down in a slow spin. There were no survivors.

Chaplain Brown in his book, Mighty Men of the 381ˢᵗ, Heroes All, says this about Bob:

"Several days have now passed since the crew went down and we have heard nothing about them. Both fliers and ground men do not cease speaking of Captain Gotthardt, one of the finest gentlemen ever to come to the 381ˢᵗ, tall, blond, good looking, loving, kindly. They tell me of his wife and four-year-old daughter whom they know. They speak of his receiving his Captaincy just a few days ago and what a fuss they made over him when he got it."

In November of 1945, after I was discharged from the service, I received a notice from the Adjutant General's Office of the War Department that I had been awarded the DFC—Bob Gotthardt's doing. In recent years I have corresponded with Bob's daughter. She was too young in 1945 to remember her father. I told her of my memories of Bob and how much I admired him.

Traveling across Holland in 1981, we stopped in Roermond. At dinner a Dutch gentleman, who had been in the Underground during the war, told us that we, as Americans, must visit the American Cemetery at Margraten, the Netherlands. The next day was the Fourth of July and we took flowers to the cemetery. I found out later that Bob Gotthardt is buried there.

In London in 1995 I had another occasion to remember Bob. At the east end of St. Paul's Cathedral beyond the choir is the American Memorial Chapel dedicated to the airmen who lost their lives flying from England. In a glass case is a large book in which is inscribed the names of those airmen. I asked a volunteer guide, Joyce, if I could see the names. She said that the case is opened only once a day when one page of the book is turned. However, she took me to a side room so I could view an exact copy of the book. I was able to verify that Robert Gotthardt's name is recorded in the memorial book at St. Paul's Cathedral.

The day that Gotthardt's crew and our crew reported to our Squadron was a Saturday. There had been a mission that day and the 533rd had lost a crew. Our greeting, as replacement crews, was less than enthusiastic. I find that it is difficult to remember my first impressions of the airbase at Ridgewell. The airfield had been built originally for the Royal Air Force. It was subsequently taken over by the 381st when the Group arrived in 1943. The field had been located like many others in the pastoral farm land of East Anglia.

The layout of the buildings on base seemed to follow no plan or logic. There were clusters of huts and buildings—quarters for officers and enlisted men, mess hall, Post Exchange, maintenance buildings, etc. The random location of the buildings on base was not by accident, but was planned and did make sense. Damage from an enemy air raid, always a possibility, would be minimized because of the dispersal of the buildings and our planes.

It was apparent that we were in for a lot of walking. The brass had access to the few jeeps. In order to get around, the crews walked or rode bicycles. From my assigned quarters one walked on a path through a grain field about a quarter of a mile to reach the mess hall. A concrete structure was our latrine (shower, sinks and lavatory) and served several nearby Nissen huts. Unheated, it was always cold and it was a challenge to time visits to coincide with the rare availability of warm water.

None of the other officers in our crew was assigned to my hut. The enlisted crews were located in a different area. The separation forced us to become acquainted with flyers from other crews. Ground personnel were not housed with air crews. Typically bunks were lined up on each side of the Nissen huts, usually with a footlocker at the end of each bunk. Except for what could be scrounged, furniture was rare. Crates or wood boxes were used to hold personal possessions. There was one small coal-burning, metal stove in the center of each hut. Coal was rationed and not of top quality. To start a fire and keep it burning was not easy, but airmen found ways to make it more flammable. Adding a small amount of napalm, a jelly-like mixture, taken from a bomb would produce a hot flame. In the cold winter of 1944-45, however, we found out that the officers' club was a much warmer place to spend an evening than our quarters.

105

As the hastily built temporary structures, many of them metal huts, became familiar to us, we adapted to them. However uncomfortable we were at Ridgewell, our living conditions were vastly superior to those of the ground troops in Europe. We had no reason to complain. When we got settled, the airbase at Ridgewell was to become our home away from home.

In the days to come the names of the nearby villages and towns would become familiar—Ashen, Ovington, Little Yeldham, Great Yeldham, Clare and Ridgewell. My favorite name was Steeple Bumstead, a village west of Ridgewell. The two Yeldhams were referred to by the airmen as Big Yahoo and Little Yahoo. The pubs in villages, like the Kings Head in Ridgewell, became places of refuge for the crews. We always felt welcomed by the local people; many became friends of American airmen.

Cambridge was about 20 miles northwest of Ridgewell. We could get there for a day traveling on a leave truck. Station 167 at Ridgewell was in Essex and probably the most southerly of all the 8th Air Force Bomber Bases in East Anglia, thus closer to London. It was easy to get there for a three-day pass. The base's proximity to London may account for the fact that we got many visiting dignitaries at Ridgewell from the military, actors, singers, politicians and royalty. Vivian Leigh, Laurence Olivier, Mary Churchill, James Cagney, Jean Neagle, Edward G. Robinson and Bing Crosby all came to the base. The actress, Mary Brian, christened the plane "Fort Lansing Emancipator." I flew it on my last mission. The actor, Robert Preston, a Special Services Officer, frequented our officers club.

My major concern during our first days on base was that they not break up our crew. We had become used to flying together and could not imagine an unknown quantity fitting into the crew.

CHAPTER 8

With the 381ˢᵗ Bomb Group

On arrival at the 381ˢᵗ I learned that my first missions would be with another crew. We flew as a crew on some practice missions, but in order for a pilot to gain combat experience, he would be assigned to fly as copilot with a veteran pilot on four missions. After those missions, our crew was to stay together during the early months of combat flying. However, after several months they started to break us up. Hugh Treadwell was sent off to train as a lead bombardier. Gene Nelson became a lead navigator. After the Eighth Air Force decided that only lead or deputy lead aircraft of a Squadron would carry bombsights, Bill Collins was trained as a toggleier. On a few occasions Rudy, Dave, Rob and Al had to fill in on other crews when an experienced airman was needed to fill a vacancy. Ellis Richard was made a first pilot and got his own crew. I was assigned to train some new pilots. I flew a couple of missions in a lead position with a mixed crew but usually had some men of our original crew. Through this entire shake up, we still thought of each other as a crew.

Our survival from the perils of combat, from our own blunders and from some questionable command decisions served to strengthen the bond of crew members. Some of our experiences with the 381ˢᵗ Bomb Group may explain why that bond has endured.

At Ridgewell our crew soon became aware of the dangers of flying a B-17 in combat. Eighth Air Force crews flew in an unfriendly environment. Usual mission altitude was between 20,000 and 30,000 feet. Over Europe in winter the temperatures could drop to 50 or 60 degrees below zero at those altitudes. Many trips to the base hospital were because of frozen extremities. A gunner who removed his gloves to clear a jammed machine gun could freeze his fingers in seconds. Condensation of breath exhaled from an oxygen mask sometimes formed into a sheet of ice on one's chest.

Anoxia from a lack of oxygen was always a threat. When leaving their stations for any reason crew members were dependent on a "Walk Around" oxygen bottle. Damage to the central oxygen system required a rapid descent to a lower, denser atmosphere. We were warned that a feeling of euphoria was a clear symptom of oxygen deprivation to the brain.

While the B-17 was a very rugged plane and could take a lot of damage, luck played a big part in a crew's survival. If a crew was shot down on a mission, "Their luck ran out", "They had it" or "Their number was up." If and when an airman finished his required missions, he joined the "Lucky Bastard Club." One time in tight formation on a mission a flak burst hit the number three engine of a B-17 flying off our left wing. The engine and wing erupted in flames and as the plane pulled away from the formation, the fuel tanks exploded. Our luck held. If our course had taken us a few feet to the left it would have been our plane going down in flames.

What follows are stories of our experiences, a chronicle of some events that remain clear in memory of our time with the 381st Bomb Group from August 1944 through February 1945.

Combat Fatigue

Fear was to become part of our existence and stress a normal condition. The psychological tests we took to qualify for flight training theoretically determined that we could handle the stress. Those tests, however, were based on probabilities. The pressure did take its toll on some airmen; it was called "Combat Fatigue."

I was ordered one day to fly with another crew to pick up and return one of our Squadron airplanes that had landed at Bury St. Edmunds, the 94th Bomb Group airfield. After landing I asked the crew about their pilot assuming he had been wounded. They told me that they were returning from a rough mission and landed at Bury St. Edmunds after being separated from the 381st BG formation. The plane did not have battle damage and there were no wounded. After they landed, however, the pilot would not get out of the plane. He just sat in the left seat on the flight deck staring straight ahead, not saying a word. He didn't react to the copilot or the rest of the crew. A flight surgeon was called. The pilot had to be carried from the plane because his legs were paralyzed. His crew didn't see it coming. Their comment was that he just cracked under the pressure. The terms "psychosomatic" or "hysteria" were not in common use then, but the paralysis must have been a reaction to the mental stress. The pilot was hospitalized. I don't think he returned to the 381st.

At the start of one mission we witnessed another incident that could have been a scene right out of the film "Catch 22." We were on the perimeter track ready to turn onto the runway behind another B-17 that was lining up for its take-off roll. Just as the plane started to move forward the waist hatch flew open. A gunner dressed in full flight gear jumped out of the plane. He ran as fast as he could across the field, across the perimeter and toward a nearby farm. The plane he had been in continued on its take-off for the mission minus one gunner. We had all heard crew members jokingly say that they had "Had it" and that they would not fly on another mission. Apparently this gunner was not joking and acting on impulse decided that he had had enough of combat flying. The Military Police probably caught him before he got very far from our airbase. Since flying was voluntary, there was usually not a court martial for those refusing to fly. The rumor was that they would be transferred to the Infantry.

The bizarre behavior of a pilot who lived in my Nissen hut was likely a reaction to the stress of combat. He talked himself into a deep depression because he thought he was being persecuted. He had decided to abort on several missions allegedly due to mechanical problems with his plane. The squadron commander had questioned the validity of the reasons he had used for aborting the missions. The pilot claimed the mechanical problems were real and were due to the fact that brass was out to get him. He convinced himself that he and his crew were purposefully assigned war-weary planes with poor maintenance records as punishment for early abortions. That was why he continued to have mechanical problems. He began to brood about his reduced chances of survival.

One night as several of us were returning from the officers club, the door of the hut flew open as I reached for the latch. It was dark so I didn't see the drunk and deranged pilot as he leaped from the door on top of me knocking me to the ground. Ellis Richard helped pull him off me and we took him into the hut. The place was a shambles. All the cots were turned over, contents of footlockers dumped, pictures torn from the walls, clothing strewn around, the Sibley coal stove was knocked over and ashes were everywhere. Photos of girl friends and wives near some bunks had been defaced. His paranoia, fueled by alcohol, had apparently turned into rage. After we quieted him down, he became very contrite and apologetic. He tearfully assisted us in cleaning up the mess. The lieutenant got through his problem, remained on flying status and, as I recall, completed his tour of combat missions with our Squadron.

R and R (Rest and Recuperation)

Such aberrant behavior, as the pilot who went berserk, was not typical. However, the unusual life style of air crews of the Eighth Air Force must have been a factor in the balancing act some flyers couldn't handle. The paradox was that an airman could be over Hamburg seeing friends blown out of the sky and that same evening be having a beer in a friendly village pub. What was the real world? Was it being in the flak over the Ruhr or with friends in Piccadilly Circus? The Brass did recognize that combat fatigue could seriously impact the prosecution of the air war, that some crew members would not be able to handle the stress. The Eighth Air Force established R and R (Rest and Recuperation) Centers for air crews. After a set number of missions, all crew members were required to take R and R leave. The American Air Force leased large manor houses from the British for this purpose. The Flyers called them "Flak Farms" or Flak Houses". When you got "Flak Happy" from flying combat, they sent you to the "Flak House." The officers from our Group went to a beautiful manor at Romsey near Southampton. The enlisted crew went for R and R to Spetchley Park, a manor house near Worcester.

The English staff of the manor at Romsey was still intact. They catered to one's very need. A very British butler came into our bedroom every morning with a tray of fresh fruit juice calling out a cheerful, "Wakie, Wakie." In addition to the regular staff at the manor, the Air Force provided an activity leader, a Red Cross employee who acted as a semi housemother. She tried valiantly to engage us in group activities, table tennis, billiards, volley ball, etc. Most of the airmen preferred to find their own amusement. I liked to relax in the paneled library, lounging in a leather chair with book in hand, sipping on a scotch and soda provided by the butler. The idea of R and R was to get our minds off the air war. I don't know if it worked, but it sure helped being treated like the Lord of the Manor.

There was an obvious difference in attitude between the fighter pilots and the bomber pilots at the R and R manor. The fighter pilots could not relax. They seemed hyperactive. They did a lot of "Hangar Flying," that is talking to each other about their flying skills, their close calls, and their victories in combat. They had been living on the edge for so long a few days R and R made little difference. They seemed eager to get back in the air.

While at Romsey our Red Cross leader arranged for a trip to Southampton so we could attend a game of American football. The game, played in a British soccer stadium, was between two U.S. service teams. One team was a U.S. Navy team (all white) and the other an Army Transportation Group team (all black). We cheered the Army team on to victory over the Navy.

The Unchecked Check List

While R and R helped get our minds off flying for a while, we were always subconsciously aware of how random were are chances of survival. It was easy to become superstitious or develop a fatalistic attitude. Some crew members would follow the same routine before every mission, i.e. some would wear the same clothes on each mission. However, with a substantial number of missions under our belts, we gained confidence. As a veteran crew we probably became overconfident, developing a more casual attitude toward flying discipline. Fortunately we had acquired a few skills that helped us to overcome some of our own mistakes. A small oversight on one of our flights could have resulted in a serious accident.

Squadron operations had directed our crew to put some time on new engines just installed in a B-17, a routine request. We would take off and fly around East Anglia for an hour. In December of 1944 the weather was horrible, with low ceilings and very cold for England. More snow or freezing rain was forecast. We trucked out to the plane, not happy with our duty on this nasty day. After hurrying through the checklist, we started engines and taxied along the perimeter to the end of the assigned runway. It had been cleared of snow. Getting the OK from the control tower, we ran up full power and started down the runway. Rudy, as usual, called out airspeed on take off. He remembers reporting speeds of 30, then 40, then 50, then 65-65-65, nothing more. I could feel our acceleration, but the air speed indicator didn't move higher. The B-17 would go airborne at about 100 MPH. I knew we were at that speed when back pressure on the controls lifted us off the runway. Then with gear up and flaps up we continued to gain speed, but the needle stayed at 65 MPH. Rudy made a quick check and reported that the pitot tube cover had not been removed.

On a B-17 G the pitot tube (which measures airspeed) is located on the left nose compartment just aft of the cheek machine gun position. On the ground the tube was covered to keep dirt out of the open end. The cloth cover had a red tag hanging down to make it more visible so you would not forget to take it off and also to avoid accidental damage to the pitot tube. The removal of the pitot tube cover was, of course, on our preflight check list and part of the "Walk Around" inspection of the plane. Our regular crew chief routinely removed the cover, but this wasn't our regular ground crew. Rudy, as our flight engineer, was embarrassed. The pilot, however, was responsible for seeing that all preflight checklists were carried out.

By immediately returning to our base we would have to admit our carelessness. Air speed could be roughly estimated by reading the engine tachometers. We needed a plan to remove the pitot tube cover before returning to the field. The pitot tube had an electrical circuit, for heat, to prevent it from icing up. I remembered that in B-17 Transition School someone had said that the cover could be burned off by turning on the pitot tube heat. We tried that tactic but could not generate enough heat in the very cold outside air to burn the cloth cover.

The next idea was to remove the small window near the pitot tube, then reach out and remove the cover. The window was held in place by about fifty screws. Rudy located the proper tool and started to work. It became apparent that removing the window would take a very long time. We then noticed that the weather was deteriorating and we were starting to pick up some ice on the wings. Without an accurate reading of our true air speed we were getting into a dangerous situation. I knew we had better get the plane on the ground. East Anglia was covered with American airfields. We spotted one, a medium bomber base for B-26's. We got into the standard pattern for a landing.

Because we didn't know our exact air speed, we needed a fast final approach to be sure we stayed above stalling speed. We came in hot! Crossing the end of the runway I cut the power, but then noticed as we touched down that a sheet of ice covered the runway. Brakes were useless. It was too late for a go-around, so I tried to keep the plane in the center of the runway hoping that we would not nose over when we reached the end of the runway. Off the surfaced runway the plane came to a stop in a field. Everything seemed OK. We hadn't mired down because the ground was frozen solid and supported the weight of the plane. Unseen from the control tower, Rudy jumped out of the forward hatch and removed the cover from the pitot tube. Using power from an outboard engine we swung our plane around and taxied back onto the perimeter track. I reported to the control tower of the airfield that we had had an ice build-up on the plane, that it was now thawed and we would take off and return to our base. Using the engines to taxi on the icy perimeter was no problem until we got back to the take-off runway and had to make a 90-degree turn. As power was applied to the left outboard engine to make a right turn, the B-17 started sliding sideways on the ice. It looked like we were going off the runway again, this time sideways. By applying power on all four engines the forward thrust straightened us out with the runway. We took off and flew below the clouds, at about 500 feet, on a direct course to our base at Ridgewell.

Not a word was said to the crew about our checklist goof up. We knew it wouldn't happen again.

Command Decisions

By late December of 1944, with about two-thirds of our required missions completed, we were considered to be a veteran air crew. As we got more missions under our belts we became increasingly aware of the risks inherent in flying in combat over Germany. While we had to accept the risks from enemy action, we hoped to avoid unnecessary hazardous situations reducing our chances of survival. We probably began to question the wisdom of some command decisions.

One such decision was the order for a maximum effort mission on 24 December 1944, disregarding a weather forecast predicting that most all of the Eighth Air Force bases in East Anglia would be fogged in when the planes returned. The Battle of the Bulge was reaching its climax. Air support was needed, but bad weather had kept the planes on the ground for days. The Eighth Air Force Commander, General Doolittle, ordered the maximum effort to bomb transportation targets behind the German lines. To the experienced crews the briefing that day sounded too much like a pep talk or maybe "Grandstanding." We were told the mission was to be a "Christmas Present for the Boys at the Front." All flyable planes of the Eighth Air Force took to the sky. In numbers it was the largest raid of the war.

The meteorologist was right. Only a few of the East Anglia air bases were clear of fog for the returning planes and they were closing down fast. Ridgewell was the only First Division base that was open. We landed, along with about 150 B-17's from various bomb groups, before our field closed down. Planes were parked on unused runways and some on muddy infields in order to keep clear one runway for landing planes. There were crash landings at or near other bases as planes tried to find airfields. I never heard how many planes crashed that day. It took several days to unscramble the mess and get the planes back to their own bases. Follow-up raids of any size could not be launched for several days. The 381st Bomb Group had thin rations for Christmas dinner on the 25th because we shared it with hundreds of unexpected guests from other Bomb Groups. General Doolittle's grand gesture did look good in print. Perhaps it was of greater value to the war effort than his "Thirty Seconds over Tokyo."

Parts of another mission that went astray are clear in my memory. Poor weather and an ill-advised plan were probably contributing factors to the foul-up on the 1 January 1945 mission. The briefed primary target was Magdeburg, not far from Berlin. Someone got the brilliant idea that if visibility was clear over England, we could get into formation at low altitude and set course for Germany in a northeasterly direction over the North

Sea, making a slow climb in route to bombing altitude. The plan was for the bomber stream to penetrate Germany in a southeasterly direction after reaching bombing altitude near Denmark. Weather recon aircraft always reported back conditions that we would likely encounter. Why the weather reports were not considered is a mystery.

Over the North Sea we came under a solid overcast of clouds, an obvious weather front. The commander of the bombers that day, instead of aborting the mission, decided to make a climb through the clouds while still in formation. The decision was passed back to the following group leaders. I could see the formations out ahead of us disappear into the clouds. Shortly after the Bomb Group ahead of us climbed into the clouds, a B-17, on its back with part of a wing missing, hit the ocean. Another plane was also in a spin heading for the sea. It appeared to me that there had been a midair collision in the clouds. Then it was our group's turn to climb into the soup. The visibility worsened as we climbed. The clouds became so dense that you could only see the one aircraft next to you in the 36-plane formation. Very wisely our group lead radioed that we would make an emergency procedure climb. This required that the outside aircraft in the formation would, on a signal, go on instruments as they made a 45-degree turn away from the heading of the lead ship. They would keep on the new heading for a given time before resuming the original heading, all the time maintaining a set rate of climb until reaching the top of the clouds. The procedure gave separation between the planes of our group. We didn't know what the other groups were doing to get through the clouds. Hundreds of planes milling around inside the clouds was a frightening thought. If I was frightened while concentrating on instrument flying, the rest of the crew must have been terrified as they searched into the mist looking for stray B-17's.

We finally broke into the blue on top of the cloud deck to an amazing sight. There were B-17's by the hundreds in the sky popping out of the clouds all around us. Lead planes were firing flares of different colors for identification and to assist in reassembling the formations. I wondered what this mess looked like on German early warning radar. Planes tagged onto any lead plane from any group as we crossed into Germany. There were formations of six planes and others looked like they had sixty. We never reached the primary target at Magdeburg. Reportedly two of our squadrons bombed Kassel, about 100 miles southwest of Magdeburg, and the lead squadron bombed Koblenz another 200 miles southwest of Kassel. In his history of the 381st, Chaplain Brown lists Kassel, Koblenz, and Itzehoe as targets for the mission. Itzehoe is about 35 miles northwest of Hamburg and a long way from Kassel and Koblenz. I don't know who bombed Itzehoe. Maybe it was our plane. I think we joined the squadron that made two bomb runs on Kassel; however, our bombs hung up. They didn't release. After leaving the target I advised the squadron lead that we still had our bombs and that we had a bombardier and bombsight available. He told us to pick a target of opportunity on the way out of Germany. We did so and were able to release the bombs. I don't know where we bombed; maybe it was Itzehoe. I don't know how many planes the Eighth Air Force lost on the mission due to enemy action or the weather. It was obvious, however, that our ragtag formations did not do much damage to the Fatherland on New Year's Day of 1945.

Prop Wash

Headquarters of the Eighth Air Force came up with a new plan. Instead of a long stream of Bomb Groups passing over the target, one after the other on the same heading, formations were going to make their bomb runs from different directions and altitudes. This plan of attack would confuse enemy radar and the aim of flak batteries. It was going to be tried on a target in the Ruhr Valley known as "Flak Alley." The plan required exact timing if the danger of midair collision was to be avoided. Each group must reach their assigned IP (Initial point of the bomb run) at the scheduled time and on the proper compass heading. Shepherding formations of 36 bombers so that they would arrive at a point over Germany on time was not an easy task for group lead navigators or pilots. Any delay would have to be made up by short-cutting of briefed routes.

The 381st was on course near enemy territory when to our amazement an entire group of B-24's crossed immediately in front of our formation, just missing our lead squadron. We were flying in the low element of the 533rd Squadron. All of a sudden the left wing went down and the plane started a steep left roll. Right aileron would not correct the roll. We were in the center of the prop wash of the B-24 group, 144 Pratt and Whitney radial engines and props churning up the sky. To avoid going completely over on our back, we had to get the nose down. We pushed the control column full forward. Before we got the plane level we had lost several thousand feet. The inability to control the plane's roll was a very scary and helpless feeling. But the roll and dive with a full bomb load proved the strength of a B-17. We probably exceeded the plane's stress limits. It was necessary to put extra power on the engines to push the Fortress back to bombing altitude and catch the formation by taking short cuts on our route.

As far as I know the plan for multiple bomb runs from different courses and altitudes was never tried again. The plan was, what the British would call, a complete cock-up. We were very lucky our plane held together.

Air Power

We did have successful missions. Most formations reached and bombed assigned targets with reasonable to excellent results. One of our crew's early missions, my eighth mission, on 17 September 1944 to Holland was an amazing example of allied airpower. The Eighth Air Force B-17's went out in small units, formations of three to six ship elements, at medium to low altitudes. Our targets were German anti-aircraft batteries and control stations in support of operation Market Garden. This was the code name for General Montgomery's plan to use airborne troops for capturing a bridge across the Rhine River at Arnheim. The 381st Bomb Group planes were assigned targets near Eindhoven, Holland. The Eighth Air Force put up 852 B-17's and four P-47 Thunderbolt Groups of about 200 aircraft to attack flak targets. After the short run across the channel to our targets, we assembled in loose formations for the quick trip back to England. The allies sent three Airborne Divisions to parachute or land by glider in Holland.

As the hundreds of Flying Fortresses and Thunderbolts crossed the channel on their return, the planes carrying the paratroops or towing gliders, and their fighter escort, were eastbound over the channel heading for the drop zones near Arnheim and Eindhoven. There were 1,550 troop carrier C-47's, about 500 gliders, British Sterling and Halifax aircraft towing gliders, escorted by more than 1,000 fighters, all heading for Holland.

In one sweeping view, from horizon to horizon, aircraft filled the sky. The total of both air armadas must have exceeded 3,500 aircraft. This awesome display of air power was a sight unlikely ever to be seen again.

Gene Nelson's diary entry for the September 17 mission was: "#8 – Einhoven, Ground Support – Beautiful Mission – No Flak – No Fighters – Invasion of Holland."

A New Copilot

After completing 15 or 20 missions we were considered a veteran combat crew. With that experience behind him a pilot was usually asked to help train newly arrived replacement pilots, taking them into combat as copilots. After Ellis Richard was made a first pilot and got his own crew, I was paired with a number of different copilots. At briefing for one mission I was told that my copilot would be a major who had been a B-17 Training Officer in the states. I had just recently been promoted to first lieutenant. I was to take the major on his first mission as my copilot. He needed the experience of some combat missions before taking on a staff position with the 381st. He made it a point to let me know how much time he had in a B-17, many more hours than I had in the "Fort." It was apparent that he felt it was demeaning to fly as copilot with a lieutenant as airplane commander.

Everything went fairly smoothly on the mission until we turned off the bomb run. The bomb bay doors would not close. The bombardier kept trying to activate the closing mechanism, but they were jammed open. An effort to manually crank the doors closed failed. I told the bombardier to keep trying, but it was quite obvious we would probably have to return to base with the doors open.

The major wanted the experience of flying formation on a combat mission. After leaving the target area and into a slow let down on our return, I told him to take over. With all of his background in the B-17, I don't think he realized how difficult it was to maneuver with the bomb bay doors in an open position. The open doors acted as additional vertical stabilizers. Along with the large vertical tail, the open doors required that the pilot use additional force on the controls to bank and turn the plane. Complete concentration was required to maintain a good position in formation. After several hours I could see the sweat on his face. I let him fly the plane until the formation approached Ridgewell. I took over for the peel off and landing. On final, air speed was reduced to about 115 MPH. Just as we were about to touch down on the runway, at about 95 MPH, the bomb bay doors closed. The closing switch had remained activated. Apparently the reduced air speed on landing had relieved some of the slipstream air pressure on the jammed doors and allowed them to close.

The major wasn't convinced. He suspected that I had conspired with the bombardier to leave the doors open so we could give him a rough taste of formation flying. Not true, but it did look very suspicious. The major had a good introduction to piloting a B-17 in combat.

The C.O. Cracks Down

Flying over Germany in a B-17 was a very dangerous profession that could drastically reduce an airman's life expectancy. Eighth Air Force flying crews learned to live one day at a time. When not on duty, they would live it up and blow off steam.

Young women from nearby towns and villages were invited to attend base dances and parties. When there was a stand-down, the officers club arranged parties. Life had been bleak for the British. Rationing had been in force for years; then here come the Americans with an unlimited supply of money, food and libido. Most young British men were off fighting the war. It was not surprising that some airmen had torrid affairs with young English women.

Many romances ended in marriage and produced the migration of British war brides at war's end. Some enterprising flyers brought girl friends on base for parties and arranged for them to stay in semi-permanent residency. They needed a place to stay. Pyramidal tents were located near crew quarters for the emergency use by new crews when waiting permanent quarters. The tents were often used by couples. One ingenious flyer put some army cots and makeshift furniture in a bomb shelter. It was not unusual to see an airman with his girl friend in the mess hall. The plentiful food served by the Air Force far exceeded the meager British diet. Some couples shacked up for several days and the young women became regulars in the mess hall.

The Commanding Officer of the 381st must have been concerned that Wing or Division Headquarters would object to what was going on. He decided there should be a crackdown on the practice. A field order was published that, in part, stated: "All female guests on base for a Friday night party or dance must be off the base by 0800 hours on the following Monday."

A Pilot's Nightmare

Most B-17 air crews were cohesive units. The enlisted crew and the officers respected and supported each other. There were, however, a few atypical crews—exceptions to the rule. I recall one air crew in our group that had a morale problem and an obvious lack of respect for each other. Pranks to relieve tension or boredom were common and in the main they were not mean or sadistic. A couple of airmen in one of our crews went over the line.

The leader of the crew, a captain, was a conscientious officer and a good pilot. I met him shortly after arriving at the 381st. He lived near Tacoma, my hometown. He had a lot of flying experience. Some on his crew resented his military demeanor and his approach to crew discipline. Unfortunately this pilot internalized the fear of combat that we all felt. After every mission he had nightmares and re-flew the mission in his sleep. He talked in his sleep giving commands to the crew and shouting warnings about flak and battle damage. Hearing about the nightmares, a couple of members of his crew thought it would be clever to frighten him awake while he was having a nightmare. He was asleep when these fellows entered the dark Nissen hut and poured a thin strip of lighter fluid on the floor around his bunk. They waited until he started talking in his sleep, lit the lighter fluid with a match, then shouted "Bail out, bail out. We're on fire!"

Waking from his sleep, momentarily believing he was in a burning plane, the pilot leaped from his bed over the flames. The pranksters thought they had pulled off a great joke and told their story about their pilot's reaction to other crews. It's a wonder that their pilot did not end up in a psycho ward after being terrorized by these airmen.

During the Korean conflict in 1950 I recognized this pilot's name in a newspaper article. He had been killed in the crash of a B-29. I wonder if his crew members ever knew what had happened to their pilot.

CHAPTER 9

Missions We Remember

Most recollections of our experiences in the air war are a jumble of events and intense feelings that can't be connected to a particular flight or date. What it felt like, those sensations, will always be with us: the vibration building up in the Fortress as throttles are pushed forward before the take-off run; the feeling of combined power when you are part of a squadron of twelve planes flying a tight, perfect formation; the fear and anger provoked by the flak and because someone down below was trying to shoot us out of the sky. But there were particular flights we can still recall in detail.

Crew members were asked to describe memorable missions they flew from Ridgewell. We each had, as Gene Nelson wrote in his diary, "a day I'll never forget." Because they were packed with unexpected and emotional events, those days stand out in our memories.

The missions described are Gene Nelson's abort with pilot Pappy Berkley on 30 October 1944, Ellis Richard's first mission on 8 August 1944, Hugh Treadwell's crash landing in Belgium on 10 January 1945, and my last mission on 14 February 1945. Rudy Staszko writes about his recollection of events on several missions.

A Day Gene Nelson Will Never Forget

Our navigator, Gene Nelson, made a short comment in his diary on each mission he flew. There is one entry for a non-mission flight. For 30 October 1944 the diary reports: "No mission, but a day I'll never forget." I asked Gene to explain this diary entry; what happened to make October 30 a day he would never forget?

On that date the 381st was briefed for a mission to Gelsenkirchen, Germany, but because of cloud cover, actually bombed the secondary target at Hamm. Chaplain Brown in his history of the 381st Bomb Group reports that all planes returned safely from that mission. That was true for the planes that reached the target. One plane had to abort and those aboard did not get credit for the mission. In October of 1944 Gene Nelson had been taken away from our crew and was flying as lead navigator. On the October 30 mission he was scheduled to fly with a 533 pilot, John W. (Pappy) Berkley. The group's formation was over Holland when Berkley's plane lost power on engine number two. Without power the propeller needed to be feathered (turned on edge into the slip stream) or it would cause excessive drag and start to windmill. Eventually the propeller shaft could tear loose and the propeller become a run-away prop. Sometimes it was impossible to feather a propeller. Because of the very low temperatures encountered at high altitude, oil for the propeller feathering system could congeal. Lead aircraft were more susceptible to this problem because they maintained fixed power settings and the oil for feathering the prop, when not in motion, would thicken. To alleviate this problem B-17's were modified in 1944. They were given an oil reserve for the propeller feathering system. We don't know if Berkley's plane had been modified.

Berkley and his copilot tried to feather the propeller on engine number two but were unable to get it feathered. With the propeller windmilling, the engine caught on fire. He aborted the mission, turning back toward England. Gene recalls that the fire spread to the wing. The propeller was running away. It tilted about 45 degrees before tearing away from the propeller shaft and the engine. Spinning off, the propeller blade sliced through the fuselage just under the navigator's station in the nose compartment.

In his recent book about the 381st, Dave Osborne reports that Berkley's engine caught fire then exploded throwing the ship on its back. The plane went into a spin and the bailout signal was given before Berkley recovered from the spin. Gene's recollection is different. He says that to extinguish the fire, Berkley gained speed in a dive then pulled the plane into a high-speed stall. This maneuver caused the plane to roll. When they pulled out of the roll they not only had lost altitude, but also they lost another engine.

They were over the North Sea when two of the crew bailed out. First Lieutenant Harry L. Delaplane, an ex Notre Dame football player, was the bombardier on the crew. He went past Gene to the escape hatch just to the rear of the navigator's position. He was part way out of the hatch when Gene noticed that he did not have his parachute chest pack. Gene handed the chest pack to him, but instead of snapping it onto his parachute harness the bombardier put it under his arm and went out the hatch. He was never seen again. Harry Delaplane is one of those listed as MIA (Missing in Action) at the American Cemetery at Maddingly near Cambridge, England.

The tail gunner, Staff Sergeant Frank K. Gunderson, also bailed out of the plane. Dave Osborne's book shows that the sergeant was killed in action on 30 October 1944 and is buried at the American Military Cemetery near Cambridge.

After losing the second engine, Berkley kept the plane flying in a slow descent, but he had to pull extra power on the two remaining engines. They were at about 5,000 to 6,000 feet when they crossed the English coast. They contemplated landing at an emergency field near the coast, but they decided to try for their home field instead. Gene gave Berkley the course heading for Ridgewell. They would make a straight-in emergency approach. On the final let down for landing, they lost the third engine. After landing and turning off the runway the last remaining engine quit.

On inspection of the plane they found that the rear of the plane was littered with rivets that had popped out of the tail section. Because of the violent maneuvers of the plane, both main wing spars had buckled. The plane was unrepairable. It was junk and probably became a hangar queen, giving up salvageable parts for other aircraft.

October 30, 1944, a day and a non-mission Gene will never forget!

Rich's First Mission

It was standard procedure that when a new crew arrived at the 381st Bomb Group both the pilot and copilot would fly their first few missions as copilot with an experienced combat pilot. After a couple of missions under their belts, they would return to fly with their original crew. A few years ago Ellis Richard (Rich), our crew's copilot, sketched out the story of his very first mission. He intended to send the final draft to the editor of the 381st newsletter, the Flyer. He never sent it; instead he gave the rough draft of his story to me.

The orders assigning our crew to the 533rd Squadron of the 381st BG are dated 5 August 1944. Ellis recalls that we reported on 7 August 1944; he could be correct. The next day, the 8th, he was assigned to fly with an experienced pilot, Lieutenant Pearce. Joseph J. Pearce had been flying combat missions since June 1944. In his story Rich mentions the lack of training for copilots at operational training units in the states. Unfortunately orders had been issued at our crew training school in Dyersburg, Tennessee, requiring that all take-offs and landings be made by the first pilot.

Also Rich comments on the incident in which bombs dropped in support of Allied ground troops fell short, causing casualties and killing a General. According to Eisenhower's book, Crusade in Europe, General McNair of the 30th Division was killed by our own bombing effort on 25 July 1944, an incident that was repeated later in the campaign. The later incident may have been on 8 August 1944. The target of the 381st on the 8th was close to the front lines at Cauvicourt, France, near Caen.

The following is Rich's letter describing his first mission:

"This is no big deal but items appearing in the August 381st Flyer brought back memories of my first mission. My crew arrived at the base August 7, 1944, and we were happy to learn that the monthly party was on for that evening. Some welcome!

"About four the next morning an orderly shook me and remarked cheerfully that I was flying with Lt. Pearce. I politely informed him that this was obviously a mistake as I had just arrived. For some reason this seemed to amuse him and he repeated his original statement.

"So I staggered in the dark to the mess and the briefing room and someone shoved me into a truck that eventually dumped me into Lt. Pearce's lap. He cheerfully informed me that we were flying left low box (or some such thing—I'm no longer sure of the nomenclature) for which reason he would be sitting in the copilot's seat. I was too groggy to argue the point, besides which I was sure that he could certainly fly the plane from either side.

"But when he cheerfully informed me, as I taxied along, that I would be taking off from the short runway, my stomach told me to give further thought to my situation. I knew something that Lt. Pearce did not: at Operational Training Unit the copilot was just a passenger until the last week when he received flight training at the controls of a B-17. My secret was that my pilot, Ed Carr, chose that time to be grounded with an ear infection, which in turn grounded the entire crew. This made for great sack time but didn't advance my skill as a pilot. Finally an instructor took me up and checked me out after three take-offs and three landings. (He didn't appear to be too interested in my welfare.)

"As our take-off moment neared, I took the philosophical viewpoint that you only die once, stomped on the brakes, gave her full throttle and let her rip. Much to my surprise, we cleared the fence at the runway and headed out.

"The mission that day was to Caen in support—at 14,000 feet—of our ground troops who were trying to break loose. It was a beautiful clear day and every direction I looked the sky was filled with little groups of our bombers, encircled by friendly fighters. To avoid dropping bombs on our own troops, no bombs were to be dropped short of a radio beacon that was directed across our flight path. Some distance from the target site, the enemy 88's were turned loose on us. The first several bursts of flak alongside our plane fascinated me. It was as though some unseen giant was blowing smoke rings at us. Everywhere I looked was the same. It appeared that each group of our planes had contracted with its own assigned 88's to lay down a lane of black top and I recalled a remark by an experienced airman at an orientation lecture that, "the flak was so thick we let down our landing gear and taxied across it." An understatement, I decided. In addition to the bursts of flak alongside, frequent lurches of the plane kept us informed of the near-bursts below the fuselage. I began to feel like a duck flying across the Colusa Gun cub marshes. Fear gripped my heart. It was only a matter of time until we would take a direct hit.

"Finally we dropped our load and headed for the friendly skies of home. But my terror wasn't quite over. There was still the little matter of landing back at Ridgewell. So I cheerfully dropped the plane in (as I had for my three practice landings at Dyersburg, and most subsequent landings at Ridgewell). Lt. Pearce cheerfully remarked, 'Good. I like a solid landing that stays put.'

"The 381st lost no planes that day, but every plane on the mission received more or less serious flak damage resulting in a stand down the following day and more sack time. I never heard whether our mission was successful but I learned from an English newspaper that some unknown plane had dropped a bomb on General _____. It was not stated whether the bomb was dropped short or whether the General was on the far side of the radio beam".

Hugh Visits Belgium

I asked Hugh Treadwell to tell me his most vivid memory of a mission he flew from Ridgewell. After some prodding from me, and no little digression from him, Hugh mentioned the 10 January 1945 mission to Cologne, Germany, when he ended up spending ten days in Belgium. The story was new to me; I had to get the details.

After 56 years I couldn't expect Hugh's memory to come up with specifics, although amazingly there were a few names and places he did recall. Basically he gave me the abridged version. The pilot of his plane was Roush of the 533rd Bomb Squadron. Hit by flak over Cologne, they made an emergency landing at an RAF Spitfire airfield near Ghent because a wounded gunner needed medical attention. The crew was housed in a school dormitory used as temporary lodging for downed airmen. It was at Zaventem near Brussels. After about ten days they were returned to Ridgewell in an RAF Dakota (a C-47 in the US Air Force.)

I have now learned a great deal more about Hugh's experiences that day and they are a lot more harrowing than he revealed to me. Dave Osborne's history of the 381st Bomb Group mentions the mission, and the 381st BG Web Site has a story of the flight by the plane's radar operator, Earl Malerich. I have talked and corresponded with the navigator, Stuart Newman, and talked again with Hugh. From these sources I have been able to piece together a fairly accurate and detailed account of what happened to Hugh's plane and crew on that mission.

Hugh had been taken away from our crew and sent to Italy for training at a school for Lead Bombardiers near Foggia. After returning to Ridgewell in December of 1944 he was assigned to fly with other pilots.

On 10 January 1945 the 381st was the lead group of the 458 First Air Division B-17's briefed to bomb Ostheim Airfield at Cologne from 25,000 feet. No one was eager to go to Cologne. We had been to the heavily defended industrial Ruhr Valley, known as Flak Alley, too many times. The weather over Europe had been bad for weeks. The plan was for lead aircraft to carry GH Radar Equipment (called Mickey) with specially trained operators who would bomb through the clouds when visual sighting by the bombardiers was not possible. The lead plane of the 381st Bomb Group was under the command of Colonel Shackley. Lt. Robert J. Roush of the 533rd Squadron was flying Deputy Lead. Because of the special GH equipment, Roush's plane on loan from the 303rd Bomb Group, carried eleven crew members. Hugh Treadwell was the bombardier on Roush's crew .

According to Osborne's book, Colonel Schackley's lead plane lost an engine before reaching the target. He was forced to jettison the bomb load in order to keep up with the formation. Roush had the difficult task of moving up to the front of the formation to take over the Group Lead. Earl Malerich, the GH operator, states that as they started the bomb run the weather cleared enough that the GH navigational and bombing equipment was not needed and the bombing was done visually by the bombardier. The radar operator would have been feeding data to the bombardier so that he could put it into the Norden Bombsight. However, with little warning, Hugh had to take over the bomb run and under extremely heavy and very accurate anti-aircraft fire, guide the Group to the bomb release point. The task was undoubtedly made more difficult because the primitive radar equipment likely did not have the plane on a precise course; thus drastic last minute corrections on the bombsight were probably required.

Turning off the target their plane was severely damaged by a direct hit and some near misses. I have a vague recollection of seeing from my position in the Group the lead plane get hit by flak. I didn't know then that Hugh was in that plane. Shrapnel tore a hole in the nose of the plane near the navigator's position. It was so close to Stuart Newman that Hugh told him to check his ass, assuming he had been wounded. Roush couldn't immediately signal that he was giving up the lead by lowering landing gear so the rest of the formation followed his damaged plane for a short time. He was not able to maintain altitude and airspeed. A large part of the tail and rudder had been shot away. Their oxygen and electrical systems were partially inoperative. The waist gunner, Staff Sergeant Arthur C. Hafner, had a severe wound to his right leg. Roush did a magnificent job of flying the damaged B-17. He had no rudder control, but slowly losing altitude they headed toward friendly territory. After three passes over an airfield, he was able to set the plane down at a small fighter base near Ghent manned by elements of the Polish RAF. Difficult to control, Roush wisely brought the plane in hot to avoid a stall. Too fast to stop, the plane went off the end of the runway into a partially frozen field. Malerich says they plowed up a frozen field of turnips before the main gear sank into the marshy ground.

Photos of the plane sitting in the snow-covered field show the extensive damage to the tail section. Only the rugged B-17 could take such damage and still fly. One photo of nine members of the crew in front of the mangled tail of the plane does not include the wounded gunner or Hugh Treadwell. I asked Stuart Newman why Hugh wasn't in the picture. He remembered that, "the tall, skinny bombardier Treadwell took the picture." A piece of the torn rudder's skin was removed and signed by the crew members.
After their landing the wounded tail gunner was rushed to the 77th British General Hospital. The rest of the crew was taken by the RAF to Zaventem near Brussels and housed for ten days in a school dormitory. Stuart Newman recalls that he was able to see the sights in Brussels and he even went to a movie.

Hugh, always aware of languages, told me that they were in a Flemish-speaking neighborhood, but most of the locals could also understand and speak some French. To pass the time they walked the streets. Children wanted to talk to the US Airmen and Hugh was able to communicate in French. They went to a small café for coffee and sometimes food. After all these years Hugh still remembers the proprietor's name, Van Malderen.

Either the RAF or the RCAF, not the US Air Force, flew Hugh and the crew back to England. First Lieutenant Robert Roush was later awarded the Distinguished Flying Cross for landing the badly crippled bomber.

Lt. Earl Malerich was also awarded the D.F.C. in part because of the 10 January mission. The whole crew deserved D.F.C.'s.

Rudy's Combat Mission Memories

I gave our flight engineer, Rudy Staszko, a difficult task when I asked him, after all these years, to write the story of one memorable combat mission. Memories are not made that way. We remember the vivid events we experienced in segments—vignettes—not usually even in the correct sequence. In his own words the following are a few of Rudy's mission memories.

"I remember the one mission where we feathered the props on engines 1 and 2, with engine number 4 vibrating and only engine number 3 running good. Dreambaby brought us back but when we went out to the flight line that evening the ground crew had all 4 engines out for replacement.

"Then there was the mission when they were tracking us just perfect. Altitude was right on the button and we had one burst behind the tail and another just in front of the nose. You conducted an oxygen check and there was no response from the nose so I put on my walk-around bottle and headed down below. A piece of flak hit Treadwell in the chest and knocked him back to the firewall. Nelson's mike became disconnected but they were both scrambling back into position. The flak vest saved Treadwell.

"I remember when the amplifier on the turbo went out someplace over the North Sea and I replaced it with the spare. Then as Tread said "Bombs away" the second amp went bad. We hit a big snowstorm and the whole formation fell apart. It regrouped again and no one was missing." (Probably Rudy is remembering the 1 January 1945 mission over the North Sea when the formation broke up during a climb through dense clouds.)

"On another mission, after having flown a couple of missions without seeing fighters, everyone was relaxed but one fighter came in from 12 o'clock level with all guns blazing and broke off to his right. Some jackass (at interrogation) reported the fighter so they asked everyone who had fired at him. There was hell to pay when they found out not one 50 cal went out to greet him.

"I remember the time we went to Keil (30 August 1944 mission) to attack the sub pens with two 2 K bombs and bombed from 32 K feet. After dropping our greeting cards we got out over the North Sea and dropped down so fast that every part of the plane had a sixteenth-inch coating of ice. On landing, the brakes locked and we were starting to go over on the nose, but you pulled back on the stick and got the tail down. The brakes made one big snap and we rolled to a safe landing."

My Last Mission, Number 35

In 1943 the tour of duty with the Eighth Air Force was set at 25 missions. With the introduction of long-range fighter protection and the declining casualty rate, the tour was extended to 30, then to 35 missions. When we arrived at the 381st Bomb Group in the summer of 1944, the tour of duty was set at 35 combat missions. After a taste of combat on our first few missions, we became aware of how hazardous each mission was, that even a milk run could result in casualties. Each of us kept count of our missions. I had a small pocket calendar and placed an X on the date of every mission. Approaching the end of the tour each of us had a tendency to sweat out each mission more than the last. I am sure each crew member remembers his last mission. I will never forget mine.

While I will not forget the significant events as they unfolded on the day of my last mission, the names of the fellow crew members with me that day were soon forgotten. This lapse of memory can be explained. No one from my original crew was on the plane. A pilot flying in the Lead or Deputy Lead positions in the formation was assigned experienced crew members from various crews. He was likely to have a different crew on each mission. His acquaintance with the crew was short, only the hours of one mission, so he didn't get to know them in non-flying situations.

The air crew with me on that last hazardous mission performed beyond the call of duty and fortunately I can now thank most of them. Dave Osborne, the 381st Bomb Group British historian must be given credit. His diligent research and amazing record keeping has provided me with interesting details of my last mission and the names of the crew. They were:

> Copilot – Rod Layton
> Navigator – Stuart Newman
> Bombardier – Jim Barrett
> Flight Engineer – Bob Pospisil
> Radio Operator – Walt Doremus
> Ball Turret – Leon Fahnestock
> Waist Gunner – John Hoene
> Tail Gunner – Joe Demski

Layton and Fahnestock were on Bob Gotthardt's original crew. I have learned that Layton passed away in 1983. Recently I have talked to both Bob Pospisil and Stuart Newman.

On 14 February 1945 we were briefed for a strike deep into Germany. The 381st was to be part of a force attacking the railroad yards at Dresden. Chemnitz was the secondary target. I was assigned to fly Deputy Squadron Lead in B-17 number 43-38983 named "Fort Lansing Emancipator." Bob Roush in B-17G number 44-8196 was flying Squadron Lead. The take-off climb to altitude and formation assembly was routine.

Over Germany, however, we ran into terrible weather. Visibility was very poor. It became difficult for the Squadron Lead to stay in formation with the group. Then we started to receive very accurate anti-aircraft artillery bursts within our formation. When you could see the bursts of flak, but could hardly see the other planes in your formation, you knew that the German flak batteries had you zeroed in on their radar. Our squadron, the 533rd, was in the trailing low squadron position of the group formation. The weather conditions had caused some formations to break up and stragglers from other groups tagged on to our squadron formation.

Next we heard on the command set that the weather would not permit bomb runs at Dresden or at Chemnitz. We didn't know it at the time, but our Group Lead, having been instructed to bomb targets of opportunity, had picked from the targets list the oil refinery at Brux, Czechoslovakia. Without warning our Squadron Lead plane turned away from the group, taking a more southerly heading. Procedure required that we stay in formation. After we had lost sight of the rest of our group, the Squadron Lead plane lowered its landing gear as a signal that the pilot was relinquishing the Squadron Lead. Battle damage was making it difficult for him to control his plane.

We moved forward in the formation and took over the Squadron Lead position. Being too far away to catch up with the group, I asked the bombardier and navigator to check the target list and select a target of opportunity that we could attack. We were probably 100 miles south of our original course to Dresden. They recommended that we make a bomb run on the Skoda Armament Works at Plsen (Pilsen) Czechoslovakia. With the stragglers we had picked up, our squadron may have totaled twenty aircraft. We made a successful bomb run on one of the largest munitions factories in Europe. The bombardier and the navigator had both done fantastic jobs getting us to the target and improvising a good bomb strike. We headed back to England. Flak damage caused us to feather a prop on one engine. By drawing more power on the other engines and making a slow descent, we maintained air speed. After a while another engine was throwing too much oil and losing power. Our fuel supply became a concern. We considered landing at an airfield near Brussels, but I believed we could get across the English Channel. Almost on empty over Ridgewell, we were losing power on a third engine when we entered the landing pattern. On final approach some crazy pilot tried to cut us out of the pattern, but we couldn't risk a go-around. He pulled away when he saw our feathered prop.

At the end of my last mission (and longest—about 91/2 hours) to have a close call on final was the last straw. Then at interrogation the intelligence officer would not believe that we had bombed the Skoda Plant at Pilsen. The Eighth Air Force Brass was worried that some aircraft may have bombed Prague, which had been declared an Open City. Thank God we had good strike photos, which when developed, verified that we had bombed at Pilsen with excellent results. The official target list for the 381st Bomb Group's mission on 14 February 1945 identifies Brux as the target. Much later it was changed to Brux/Pilsen.

It had been a tradition in the earlier days at the 381st BG for a pilot to buzz the field, making a fly-by on the deck, when returning from his last mission. Occasionally a pilot would still disregard orders prohibiting this dangerous practice. Returning on my last mission I never considered the possibility of a buzz job. I guess I was too concerned about getting the plane on the ground in one piece. On the ground and taxiing to our hard stand the thought came to my mind that I would not have to fly from Ridgewell again. Reaching our hardstand, I swung the plane around by touching the left brake as the throttle to the right outside propeller was advanced. I cut the engines, the props stopped, and then silence. It didn't sink in. This was the last time I would be at the controls of a B-17. As we climbed out of the plane for the last time the feelings I had cannot be described as elation—more a general sense of relief and well-being that I had made number 35!

CHAPTER 10

The British Connection

Most Eighth Air Force bases were located in East Anglia. Although surrounded by farmland the air bases, because of security requirements, were small islands of America. To meet the British we had to go off base. On our first leave we didn't know what to expect. Neither did the locals. Many impressions of Americans came from Hollywood movies. Short trips to nearby villages—Ridgewell, Great Yeldham, Ashen, and Ovington— gave us a chance to get acquainted. In the pubs, like the Kings Head in Ridgewell, we were able to meet some of the regulars. Dave Phillips talks fondly of some folks from Ridgewell, Nelly and Sam Warren. They took him into their home and he stayed with them when on pass. They became close friends.

I think the spirit of the British amazed us all. Even after five years of war they remained optimistic and very determined to keep up the effort. The largest town on the road from Ridgewell to Cambridge was Haverhill. On one occasion several of our crew took the leave truck to Haverhill and decided to take in a movie. During the show the manager walked on stage to announce that an air raid alert had been sounded and that V-l Buzz Bombs were expected in the area. He asked if the audience wanted him to stop the movie so they could take shelter until the all clear was given. The unanimous opinion expressed was to continue with the movie. No one left the theater and the show went on. A short time later we heard and felt a large explosion. A Buzz Bomb had impacted nearby. The manager again appeared on stage and got the same answer, "Go on with the film."

It was a delight to meet and talk to the children. Too young to have acquired British reserve, they called us "Yanks." A typical greeting was, "Any gum, chum?" They knew we usually carried gum or candy from the Post Exchange when going off base. On the morning train from Yeldham toward Colchester we often encountered a group of children boarding the train for their trip to school. I don't recall where they got off the train, probably at Halstead. Their chatter was typical of grammar school children, but they were still polite and considerate of one another and of the other train passengers.

Trains provided an opportunity for us to meet and talk to people. On a trip back to Ridgewell from London I sat opposite a little gray haired lady. I remember that she quizzed me all the way about my home and family. What a great pleasure it was to talk to her. The East Anglians we met near our base at Ridgewell were mostly straight-talking farm people.

The Londoners were a different breed, but no less friendly. In our time in the great city we saw the terrible damage inflicted by the London

Blitz. The bombing had left great scars and gaps in the row houses and buildings of London. During the Blitz the German bombers targeted the docks on the Thames for destruction. On the south side of the river, about two miles east of the Tower Bridge, the Rotherhithe region of docks and surrounding residences received heavy bombing. The air raids caused great destruction and many casualties. To honor the dead, the injured, and the survivors of Rotherhithe a new plane assigned to our Squadron, the 533rd, was named "Rotherhithe's Revenge." It was B-17G number 42-31761. Assigned to the 533rd BS early in 1944 the plane became somewhat of a legend. Chaplain Brown flew in the "Revenge" in March of 1944 on the first of his five missions. He was the only group chaplain to fly on combat missions. As I recall we flew Rotherhithe's Revenge a couple of times. The plane had over 73 missions and survived the war.

The V-2 ballistic rockets, with their large warhead, were still being launched by the Germans. We saw the destruction they caused in London. When the city was under attack from rockets, many Londoners were still taking shelter in the tunnels of the Underground Stations. Their courage and determination was remarkable. Spotting our Air Force uniform, many a Londoner would flash Churchill's famous V for Victory sign.

It was easy to get lost in London's maze of streets. Always helpful, the citizens would give detailed instructions in reply to any request for directions. Then they would invariably add, "You can't miss it!" The cab drivers of London were uncanny in their ability to reach a destination in the fog, in a night black-out and with headlights mostly covered with black paint—blind flying at its best.

Many of the young women of England were in military service or working in vital war industries outside of London. Those left in London mostly worked in business or government offices. They seem to be having a wonderful time. London was swarming with Allied military personnel nearly all on leave and with money to spend. Intense competition to meet or date a young lady could become quite cutthroat. In Shepard's Pub, a haven for young officers, it was very foolish to leave a date alone at a table even for a quick trip to the W.C. Immediately she would be the center of attention by a lieutenant on the loose eager for a date. Sometimes it was apparent from her clothes if a young woman was dating an American Army Officer. The Post Exchange in London sold the wonderful heavy twill material used for officer's pants (referred to as "pinks"). With cloth very scarce, a young lady wearing a skirt or suit made from the "pinks" material obviously had acquired it from an American boy friend.

London tailors could make anything with the right cloth. My garrison hat had been taken from a rack in a London pub. I found a hatter on Bond Street. Instead of buying a replacement at the Post Exchange, I ordered one custom made. The hatter took measurements of my head with a strange looking device and promised to produce a final product in a few days. It turned out to be the best garrison hat I had ever worn, a perfect fit and light weight. The proprietor assured me that in case I needed another hat, my head measurements would be filed in their records for life.

London could be gray, wet and cold. The winter of 1944-45 was one of the worst in many years. The Continent was in a deep freeze in December and January. England didn't escape the cold and snow. The homes and flats of London were still mostly heated by coal and coal was rationed. When we were invited into a London home, the host always would get a fire going using part of their precious supply. They also shared what food they had and greatly appreciated any gift of food or sweets. If the Londoners could ignore the miserable winter weather, how could we complain?

In London or in the villages of East Anglia, we always felt welcomed by the British. In various ways we each made our own connection with them. As far as we can determine one of our crew, Bill Collins, returned to Britain, married and is still there.

CHAPTER 11

A Tale of Four Fortresses

On the front and back covers of this book are copies of two colored photographs of B-17's of the 381st Bomb Group in flight over the fields of East Anglia. The planes can be identified as belonging to our squadron, the 533rd, by the letter VP painted on the fuselage. The photographer's name is unknown, but he was an Army Air Force photographer flying with our bomb group. Because there are both camouflaged and silver B-17G's in the pictures, and one of the planes went down in late September of 1944, I believe the photos were probably taken in the summer of 1944.

Using the research done by Dave Osborne for his book, They Came From Over the Pond, it was possible with the serial numbers to track down the fate of four of the planes in the two photographs. We knew the crews that flew these planes and shared in their fate. Our crew was very familiar with one of the planes, the only one that survived the war.

One of the photographs, the one with plane No. 232025(P) in the foreground and No. 231570(W) in the background, was on the cover and inside of the book, An Illustrated History of the Air Forces of World War I and World War II, by Chant. No. 025(P) was called "Dreambaby" and No. 570(W) was "Lucky Me."

The other color photograph with B-17 No. 297503(X) in the front and No. 237791(V) behind it was in the March 1945 issue of the National Geographic Magazine. No. 503(X) was known as "Princess Pat", but No. 791(V) was unnamed. At my request the National Geographic sent me prints of this photo. One of these prints I gave to the Kings Head Pub in Ridgewell in 1983, as part of the Pictures for Pubs Program of the Eighth Air Force Historical Association. The proprietor, Steve Worth, showed the picture to a few of the pub regulars who were having their daily pint. The discussion provoked by the picture was fascinating to hear. The elderly gentlemen disagreed on the location of the photos and tried to identify villages by the shapes of farm fields and roads.

Three of the four planes went on the 200th mission of the 381st Bomb Group to Schweinfurt, Germany, on 9 October 1944. The mission plan sheet for that day shows that Bob Gotthardt and his crew led the low element of the 533rd Squadron in plane No. 791(V). Our crew was in No. 025(P), Dreambaby, on his right wing. The letter B next to our plane indicates that we were to monitor the fighter-bomber radio channel for the squadron. Plane No. 503(X), Princess Pat, was piloted by Windsor and flew on the left wing of the Squadron Lead plane. All of the group's planes returned safely from Schweinfurt that day.

B-17 No. 231570(W) did not go to Schweinfurt on 9 October. Lucky Me had been unlucky on an earlier mission. On its 65th mission 25 September 1944 to Frankfurt, Germany, that aircraft piloted by Lieutenant Gill was seen to go down over the target area. All of the crew bailed out and spent the rest of the war in POW camps.

B-17 No. 237791(V) met its fate in December of 1944. Lieutenant Pearce was the pilot of No. 791 on the 9th of December. The target, Cologne, was always heavily defended as it was in the heart of the industrial Ruhr Valley. Over the target the plane suffered severe battle damage and developed engine trouble. Pierce was able to make a forced landing in Belgium. The crew walked away from the plane, but it did not fly again. It was placed on salvage status on 5 January l945.

B-17 No. 297503(X), Princess Pat, suffered an ignoble end at Ridgewell. On 26 March 1945 the 381st went to Zeitz where accurate flak caused extensive battle damage to the planes. Returning to base, Princess Pat made a crash landing and was destroyed by fire. The aircraft was scrapped.

B-17 No. 232025(P), Dreambaby, was our crew's favorite plane. It was still flying with the group after our crew members had completed their combat tours. Dreambaby returned to the U.S. in June of 1945. That wonderful plane ended up with hundreds of other B-17's at the bone yard in Kingman, Arizona, in December of 1945. The planes there were eventually cut up for scrap metal. But we will all remember Dreambaby. That plane deserves its own story.

CHAPTER 12

Dreambaby

After 38 years I returned to Ridgewell in 1983. Gene Nelson with Ellis and Robin Richard had attended the dedication of the 381st Memorial the year before. In August I drove from London to Ridgewell. I stayed in a hotel in Cavendish and the next morning drove on a farm road toward Ridgewell. Coming to a turn, I recognized that I was driving on the perimeter track of Air Station 167. I visited the 381st Memorial at Yeldham and the Kings Head Pub at Ridgewell. My travels took me to the American Military Cemetery at Maddingly where I saw the names of 381st airmen buried there. Then at Duxford I visited the Royal Air Force Air Museum. The gift shop displayed a poster of all U.S. aircraft of World War II. The B-17 illustrated on the poster was Serial Number 42-32025, Triangle L on the tail for the 381st Bomb Group, VP on the waist for the 533rd Squadron and the letter P to identify the plane named "Dreambaby". Our crew had flown Dreambaby on more of our missions than any other B-17. Of course I bought a poster.

In 1984 I heard about the planned celebration of the 50th anniversary of the first flight of the B-17. The Boeing Company was going to host in 1985 reunions in Seattle of the Air Force units that had flown the Flying Fortress. I decided to do some research on the B-17. In the Seattle Public Library I came across Roger Freeman's book, B-17 Fortress at War. A color photograph taken in the summer of 1944 of Dreambaby flying over East Anglia was reproduced in the book. The same photo was on the front jacket and inside of Chant's book, Air Forces of World War I and II. I also found that a painting of Dreambaby was used as the front piece for the Time-Life book, America in the Air War. At an Aircraft Art Gallery near Boeing Field (King County Airport) I found a poster for the Smithsonian's Air and Space Museum exhibit of 1983-84. It was a painting of a B-17 by British artist, Frank Wooten,—Dreambaby again.

Why Dreambaby out of all the 12,731 B-17's built? I found out later that Dreambaby with over 1000 combat hours and 73 missions, had survived the war. It was the first silver B-17G (without camouflage paint) to be delivered to the 381st BG. The plane was assigned to the 533rd BS on 21 February 1944. Stuart Watson's crew got No. 025 when it was new. Watson's wife was expecting a baby so his crew chose the name Dreambaby in honor of their pilot's unborn child. Watson later became C.O. of the 533rd Bomb Squadron. Because a single silver B-17 stood out in a formation, it was decided to apply camouflage paint to the plane thus making it a less apparent target for enemy fighters. I have been unable to find out who designed and painted the nose art on Dreambaby, a shapely ghost-like female figure, under the pilot's window.

Not all B-17's flew the same. Dreambaby was particularly good to fly. It was easier to trim and seemed to respond better than other B-17's to the flight controls. I don't think that Dreambaby ever aborted a mission due to mechanical problems. The crew chief and his ground crew must have been one of the best at the 381st.

Forty years after we had flown the plane, the reappearances of old No. 025 in photos and paintings began haunting me. I wrote a too-long poem about a combat mission over Germany in Dreambaby. It was written in 1985 before the Seattle reunion of our crew.

Dreambaby

Called by a dream of an aircrew and their B-17
Airbase at Ridgewell, all still clearly seen,
Sleep the healer, those nights of forty-four
From the nightmares of violent air war.

Footsteps are heard in the Nissen hut night
Turn in your bunk to avoid the light
Orderly's voice, the beam finds your eye,
Whispers your name, "You're scheduled to fly."

Men stir in bunks; tired bodies come alive
Breakfast O-Four hundred; briefing set for five
Cold water, cold shave, so mask will fit tight
Oxygen needed in high altitude flight.

In darkness file up the path to the mess
Powdered eggs, spam, breakfast more or less
Vibrations are felt, rough engine on a Fort
Ground crews working to prevent an abort.

At briefing hear details of today's mission
Which plane we'll fly, our formation position
025 our ship, low squadron, low flight
Flying as wingman on Gotthardt's lead right.

Stations, start, taxi, plus weather, routes, flak
Covered at briefing before final time hack
Winter flying garb; we sweat walking to the truck
Drive the perimeter through damp October muck.

At hardstand ready waits 025 our plane
Loaded with bombs, filled with high octane
Nose art a figure, curvaceous form in white
Ghostly lady, Dreambaby's all right.

Fuselage and wings of olive drab shade
Oil stains and dents mark our war-weary maid
Patches cover holes from Magdeburg, Frankfurt
Munster, Cologne, Merseburg, Schweinfurt.

Will we scrub or go? The usual apprehension
Banter with line chief eases air crew's tension
Push through each fan, pulling oil to the top
Less wear a difference for Wrights about to stop

Preflight checks done; time for stations near
 Crewmen at positions check survival gear
Headsets, mikes, masks; harnesses, flak vests,
Escape kits, helmets; parachutes, Mae Wests.

 Collecting extra vests for use as armor mail
Tail gunner's pill box weighs down the tail
Waist gunner helps unload the extra freight
Slowly time passes; we have only to wait.

Start engine time's here; you hit number three
Coughs once or twice before heeding your plea
Four radials alive; Dreambaby's props spin
With thirty-five others wakes Ridgewell with the din.

Wing, Division, Eighth; a thousand times four
Spread the Cyclones'chorus across Anglia's floor
At taxi time, our bird leaves its nest
To parade the perimeter with all the rest.

Flares signal go; the first Fort rolls by
Taxiing in line, pilots wait turns to fly
Dreambaby wheels round; we line up with care
Watching planes ahead struggle into the air.

Concentrate in cockpit; apply full take-off power
Engineer calls air speed as we race past the tower
Eighty, ninety, hundred, straining against every pound
At runway's end our girl leaves the ground.

Another take-off; copilot's voice comes through
His calm "Gear up!" gives confidence to crew
Into dense overcast, instrument climb at steady rate
Needle mustn't vary; air collisions seal your fate.

Altimeter shows we've climbed up to ten
Pilot signals crew; time to go on oxygen
Brightness above; we break into the blue
Relief now on top to admire the sunlit view.

Over cumulous tops the Eighth displays its might
A thousand Forts assembled; we're awed by the sight
Aircraft fill the sky; contrails in every direction
Gathering into Groups, formations for protection.

Cutting across the arc to Group lead on the right
Under low element and up into our flight
In with silver Gees, Dreambaby looks out of place
Drab paint's no match; will she keep up the pace?

She flies on easy step responsive to each control
Stays in level flight; suspect she has a soul
Armada moves over green patch fields below
Leaves England's coast at checkpoint Felixstowe.

Gunners test fifties when over mid channel
Jarring recoil shakes every rivet and panel
Cordite's acrid smell entering each oxygen mask
Confirms gunners are ready for their task

Crossing into Holland; see some puffs of black
Eighty eights on range; Libs attracting lots of flak
Five miles high the Fortress really soars
Poor bastards below catching hell in Twenty-fours.

Rivers, fields, roads; Europe in clear outline
Eastward we move; now we're past the Rhine
Defenders now know our intended bomb strike
A primary target deep within the Reich.

Turning from IP, start a long bomb run
Direct course flown to get the job done
No urging needed; formations close in tight
Knowing what happens in straight level flight

Dense cloud ahead of the deadly black stuff
Looks like they're throwing up more than enough
Fly into flak; bursts missing by inches
On to the target; Dreambaby never flinches

Near in our Group a Fort's wing is on fire
Flame streaming back; one big funeral pyre
Danger to the rest, she turns away in a glide
No one bails out from that crew's last ride.

Hold formation close; with prop wash we contend
An eternity passes; will the run never end?
Bombs away from our lead; we salvo on the sight
Pregnant weight released; Dreambaby lifts up light.

Delivered the load, empty bomb bay
Move off this course; get the hell away!
Nose down for speed; into a tight turn
Evade the barrage; let stragglers return.

 Check on the crew from tail, waist, ball,
Radio, turret, nose; O.K.'s from them all
Survey damage; we've been really battered
With power and control; her ruggedness mattered.

Headwinds cut our speed; covering little ground
Too long over Fatherland; yet homeward bound
Then slow descent and we begin to feel
The end's in sight; chance of survival real.

Tension to euphoria on final let-down
Oxygen masks off; crew starts to clown
On intercom tail gunner's voice is heard
A country tune, "The Great Speckled Bird."

Over white cliffs, under clouds of slate
Rejoicing we made it in this beloved crate!
Fields, hedgerows, steeples, roofs of red,
Villages with pubs, Ridgewell there ahead.

Peel off to left; mission end is near
On downwind leg lower landing gear
No flares, no wounded; Dreambaby's come through hell
Again we touch down in the best of Triangle L.

Designed for strength and line, graceful fin held high
Awkward on the ground but beautiful in the sky!
The one that got us back; most clear in recollection
Dreambaby's the Fortress we remember with affection.

The men who flew her are not inclined to boast;
To them and to Dreambaby this past-due toast:
To this courageous crew I'd like to lift my glass
Honoring them all and our Boeing-born lass.

And here's to the others who never got back
The Forts and men downed by fighter or flak
Empty bunks in huts; four engines now mute
Fragments of dreams, deserving silent salute.

CHAPTER 13

Ridgewell to the ZI (Zone of Interior)

A tradition on the day an officer flew his last mission was a celebration at the officers club. I am sure the sergeants had a similar blast. At the 381st the drinks were free for the honored guest. The bar at Ridgewell was L-shaped. At the inside corner of the L was a parachute harness bolted to the bar. On arrival you were escorted to the bar and strapped into the parachute harness. It was supposed to support you if too many free drinks were consumed. Our bartender had come up with a concoction he called the V-2. He filled a large milk shake sized glass with ice and then went across his line of bottles pouring a jigger from each into the glass. To kill the awful taste of the mixture, and make it drinkable, he topped it off with cherry brandy. It almost tasted like a cherry coke. I finished two of these concoctions. Some friends helped me back to my quarters and into a bunk for a sound and deep sleep.

It took several days after my 35th mission on 14 February 1945 for the fact to sink in. An orderly would not be shaking me awake before dawn for another mission. I was a lame duck, superfluous to the purposes of my squadron and the group. And the administrative office acted fast. Our Group Commander, Lt. Col. Conway Hall, certified on the 14th that my operational tour of duty as a pilot and a member of a combat crew on B-17 aircraft was completed. The certification recommended that I be reassigned to further combat in another theater after a period of rest in the ZI (Zone of Interior).

Special Order No. 46 was issued on 15 February transferring me, along with four other 1st lieutenants and a staff sergeant from the 381st Bomb Group to the 70th Replacement Depot (Station 591). None of the members of my original crew were listed; they had not completed their tour on the same date. The Special Order stated that, "Pers will rpt on earliest practicable date subsequent to presentation of all DFC and AM (and/or recommended or in the process of being recommended, pers to be retained not in excess of ten (10) days), to await ret to ZI." It was during these few days that I was interviewed and recommended for the DFC.

I was cleared as still on flying status by our Flight Surgeon, Captain Graham, and Squadron Commander, Captain Watson, on 17 February. I turned in my personal flying equipment to squadron supply on the same day. A shipping ticket for equipment in my possession dated 19 February 1945 suggests that I departed from the 533rd Bomb Squadron and Ridgewell on that date.

The 70th Replacement Depot was located near Liverpool, about half way between that port and Manchester. As I recall we traveled by train to the new station. Three boring weeks were spent waiting for shipping orders for my return to the States. Most of us at the Depot hoped to get on an Air Transport Command plane. To pass the time I was able to visit some of the nearby towns. Compared to rural East Anglia with its picturesque villages, the Manchester area was depressing. We were now located in the industrial heart of England. In the town of Wigan there seemed to be endless bleak streets of small, red brick row houses of the factory workers.

Time passed slowly and many of the flyers joined in the round-the-clock poker games. Figuring that I had used up my share of luck flying in combat, I didn't play. The pot in some of the games consisted of high stacks of five-pound notes. Most of the players, lieutenants, were tossing the English notes into the pot as if they were US dollars. At the exchange rate in 1945 a five-pound note was worth over $20. Many of the poker players were going to arrive home flat broke.

We finally learned we would travel by ship from Liverpool. Our ship was the New Amsterdam, a Dutch ship that was reportedly the fourth largest passenger liner in the world. It had been at sea when the Germans invaded Holland. In 1945 the Dutch crew was still operating the ocean liner as an Allied Troop Transport. We sailed from Liverpool for New York on 13 March 1945. The large, faster ocean liners, the Queen Mary, the Queen Elizabeth and the New Amsterdam, did not travel in convoy but made solo crossings of the Atlantic. The ship was crowded with returning troops. On our first day at sea we were assigned to specific tables and times to eat in the large dining room. Our Dutch waiter was a gem. At our first meal he instructed all officers at his table to arrive for every meal, eat our food, and no one would miss a meal. He would guarantee that none of us would be seasick during the voyage, which was always very rough in March. I think there were seven or eight at the table. We all followed his orders. At each meal in following days there were fewer in the dining room. By the third day at sea the room was almost empty except for our full table. It was a rough crossing, but none of us missed a meal and none of us got sick.

On 17 March 1945, exactly two years since I had arrived in San Francisco from Hawaii to join the Air Force, we sailed into New York harbor. Numerous small craft, including a fireboat, greeted the New Amsterdam as it passed the Statue of Liberty. We were all on deck watching the scene. The fireboat was sending streams of water in the air and blaring music from loud speakers. Maybe we were expecting patriotic music. What we got was the Andrews Sisters singing "Rum and Coca Cola"! No matter. We were eager to hit the streets of New York. The ship docked at a Manhattan pier. We were then advised that we would be confined to the ship overnight and in the morning transported to Fort Dix, New Jersey, for processing. Those in command must have realized that once "on the town" in New York we might not get to Fort Dix for many days. Our first night back in the ZI was spent on the deck of the ship grumbling as we admired the lights of New York City around us, but we were back in the USA!

CHAPTER 14

Bill Boeing's Brand

At the urging of Dave Osborne, co-author of the book <u>The B-17 Flying Fortress Story,</u> I am including the following story in this narrative. The story does not relate to our air crew, but it does have a connection with the plane we flew, the B-17.

First some background information to set the scene. In 1929 the Boeing Company and Pratt and Whitney, manufacturer of aircraft engines, had merged forming United Aircraft and Transport Corporation (UATC). They acquired Stearman Aircraft Company and several airlines, uniting them as United Air Lines. William Boeing, Sr., the founder of the Boeing Company, was chairman of UATC. He intended to retire at age 50 in 1931, but stayed on for three more years.

Senator Hugo Black of Alabama instituted hearings in January and February 1934, on the methods used by the postmaster general in granting airmail contracts to the airlines. Bill Boeing testified at the hearings about the risks and hazards of the aviation industry and that he had risked his personal fortune to build aircraft and fly the mail. Black obtained a decree from the postmaster general that the large airlines could only retain airmail business by reorganizing into separate entities. Subsequently Congress passed a law that no airline could be associated with a manufacturer of aircraft or aircraft engines.

Bitter about the break-up, Bill Boeing in 1934 sold all of his stock in UATC and retired from the company. He had vast timberland holdings in Washington and Oregon from his earlier days in that business. Eugene Rodgers in his book, <u>Flying High</u>, says that Boeing, "true to his resolve spent most of the rest of his life as a country gentleman. Breeding cattle and horses and sailing his yacht on Puget Sound." The same year that Bill Boeing retired the Boeing Company was starting a very risky enterprise, the design work on the first heavy multi-engine bomber that was to become the B-17 Flying Fortress. It first flew on 28 July 1935.

William Boeing lived at his home in the Highlands north of Seattle until the start of World War II. In 1942 he moved to his 1000-acre farm about 20 miles east of Seattle near Preston. It was rumored that he wanted to get away from Seattle in the event it was bombed by the Japanese; however, after Pearl Harbor he offered to return to the company without pay in order to help with the war effort. He served as an advisor to the company's president and drove his pickup truck several times a week from the farm to the Boeing plant.

In 1943 Bill Boeing started to raise cattle on the farm. His aim was to improve the quality of livestock, particularly Hereford cattle, in the northwest. At various times they raised beef and dairy cattle, sheep, and pigs on the farm. In the mid 1990's I met the manager of the Boeing farm, Bud Abbot, through my brother. Bud's father, a horse expert, had started working for Bill Boeing in 1927. Bud, after serving in the navy and graduating from Washington State University, took over the management of the farm in 1951. In the late 1990's the Boeing family decided to sell the farm. A golf course and 270 homes are being built on the land. In preparation for the sale, Bud Abbot was clearing out and disposing of old farm equipment from the barns. Because The Abbots knew I had flown B-17's Bud presented me with one of Bill Boeing's original branding irons.

.

To identify his cattle William Boeing had registered his brand in 1943 as "B-17" because that airplane had made the Boeing name famous. The branding irons were made in three sizes and one of them was electric. The brand B-17 was registered to William Boeing for five years and renewed twice in 1948 and 1953. Bill Boeing died in 1956 while on board his yacht. The brand registration was not renewed after his death. With 17 miles of fence enclosing the farm there was little likelihood that the cattle could stray.

Because of what the B-17 meant to flyers and what it symbolizes for the Boeing Company, the Air Force and the Pacific Northwest, the branding iron I have is a treasured artifact. A tracing of the B-17 brand and a photograph of the branding iron are shown with the text.

The branding iron has been donated to the Museum of Flight in Seattle, where it is on display with the story of Bill Boeing.

HEADQUARTERS   C-F-3
ARMY AIR FORCE STATION 112
APO 639

SO 217.   E X T R A C T   4 Aug 1944

1. Fol O & EM ACU & atchd to 1st Repl & Tng Sq (B) are trfd to orgns indicated o/a 5 Aug 1944; EM (*) on TD at AAF Sta 172 WP to respective orgns upon completion of tng at AAF Sta 172. GMV/Rail. TCNT TDN. 60-136 P 414-01 A 212/50425.
Auth: TWX D-67332, Hq Eighth AF, 3 Aug 1944. (‡ Officer in Charge)
Class "K" rat are auth for O & EM while on travel status only.

CREW AF-51 (FP900BA/16305BA-33/33)	TO: 381ST BOMB GP, AAF STA 167
2D LT CARR, EDWARD C. 01080093‡(P)	2D LT RICHARD, ELLIS E. 0714568 (CP)
2D LT NELSON, EUGENE L. 0723149 (N)	2D LT TREADWELL, HUGH W. 0708027 (B)
Sgt(757)Hines, Albert D. 35608948	Sgt(748)Staszko, Rudolph S. 37469124*
Cpl(611)Collins, William J. 33600428*	Cpl(611)Lamp, Glenn L. 15174303*
Cpl(611)Phillips, David A. 31399137*	Cpl(611)Whitaker, Robert W. 35697441*
CREW AF-53 (FB333CJ/16209CJ-187/187)	TO: 381ST BOMB GP, AAF STA 167
2D LT GOTTHARDT, ROBERT J. 0765248 (P)	2D LT LAYTON, RODNEY M. 0824145 (CP)
2D LT SCOONES, EDGAR G. 0718434 (N)	2D LT STEPHENS, ROBERT O. 0769226 (B)
Cpl(757)Ellingham, Donald J. 36657893	Sgt(748)Norman, Howard M. 17065516*
Cpl(611)Bailey, Edward B. 35875498*	Cpl(611)Baird, David T. 37501610*
Cpl(611)Bishop, Richard A. 35228764*	Pfc(611)Fahnestock, Leonard L. 33544109*
CREW AF-54 (FB333CJ/16209CJ-240/240)	TO: 381ST BOMB GP, AAF STA 167
2D LT FULTON, OMAR P. 0820989 (P)	2D LT HARRINGTON, ROBERT B. 0768537 (CP)
2D LT CONLY, ROBERT X. 0723293 (N)	Sgt(612)Berry, Franklin S. 37154192*
Pvt(757)Martin, Roger A. 36598127	Sgt(611)Von Goeben, Carl J,Jr. 20241492*
Sgt(611)Hill, Charles W. 16072941*	Sgt(748)Jefferson, Theodore L. 19124659*
Pvt(611)Grubbs, James C. 35583739*	
CREW AF-55 (FB333CJ/16209CJ-227/227)	TO: 381ST BOMB GP, AAF STA 167
2D LT SCHOLZE, ROBERT P. 0555452 (P)	F/O GREGOIRE, GORDON G. T-61988 (CP)
2D LT FOSTER, JAMES R. 0717643 (N)	2D LT McGILVRAY, JAMES M. 0769337 (B)
Cpl(757)Freestone, Marion M. 17152381	Sgt(748)Bonham, Dorin A. 18084618*
Sgt(748)Fettus, Robert D. 6281522*	Cpl(612)Kay, Gale H. Jr. 17056028*
Cpl(611)Pomeranke, Glen C. 37671226*	Cpl(611)Schnitker, Leo J. 37476470*
CREW AF-58 (FB333CJ/16209CJ-230/230)	TO: 381ST BOMB GP, AAF STA 167
2D LT MITCHELL, RICHARD A. 0555306 (P)	F/O BOONE, RAY. T-62312 (CP)
2D LT ARNOLD, JAMES F. 0723265 (N)	2D LT AVERY, FRED H. 0708063 (B)
Sgt(757)Trainor, William J. 15171246	Sgt(748)Dungan, Leo J. Jr. 38406030*
Sgt(612)Hermel, Howard A. 37565345*	Sgt(748)Macklin, Harold P. 37526140*
Sgt(611)Sapienza, Clarence C. 36475065*	Cpl(611)Hall, Glenn W. 35807165*
CREW AF-52 (FD333RJ/16212RJ-92/92)	TO: 91ST BOMB GP, AAF STA 121
2D LT ERNST, ARTHUR. 0761060‡(P)	2D LT FREER, DONALD R. 0710914 (CP)
F/O KOVANDA, JAMES H. T-125757 (N)	2D LT STRAUSS, LEWIS Z. JR. 0772768 (B)
S/Sgt(757)Smith, Alva E. Jr. 18115429	S/Sgt(748)Garner, Alvis O. 18120945*
Sgt(612)Craft, Herbert L. 33569267*	Sgt(611)Davis, William E. 37622854*
Sgt(611)Hinz, Clarence R. 36832271*	Cpl(611)Herczeg, Frank F. 36166204*
CREW AF-56 (FB333CJ/16209CJ-228/228)	TO: 91ST BOMB GP, AAF STA 121
F/O YAVIS, JOHN J. T-61740 (P)	F/O EDWARDS, EMERY L. JR. T-62315 (CP)
2D LT ANNES, JOHN J. 0723259 (N)	2D LT SCHWARZ, HENRY A. 0762872 (B)
Sgt(757)Sikorski, Eugene C. 33136142	Sgt(748)Anderson, Homer C. 17127927*
Sgt(612)Doran, Joseph P. Jr. 33438419*	Sgt(748)Johnson, Fines L. 38343596*
Cpl(611)Davenport, Thornwell E. 14181450*	Cpl(611)Mueller, Vernon L. 33388007*
CREW AF-57 (FB333CJ/16209CJ-229/229)	TO: 91ST BOMB GP, AAF STA 121
F/O LINDAHL, JOHN R. T-62050 (P)	F/O CATER, JOSEPH J. T-62136 (CP)
2D LT ARAKAS, ADAM. 0723263 (N)	2D LT WEINSTOCK, JOSEPH G. 0755136 (B)
Cpl(757)Simone, Frank J. 33411945	Sgt(612)Algee, Leslie D. 19090491*
Sgt(748)Beach, Vincent M. 39277275*	Cpl(748)Barclay, John W. 38419547*
Cpl(611)Mancino, Arthur R. 35231377*	Cpl(611)Paster, Robert M. 35917645*

```
SPECIAL ORDERS  )                                    HEADQUARTERS AAF STATION 167,
NUMBER    175  )                                       APO 557      5 August 1944.
```

1. Fol O & EM, having been asgd this sta per par 1, SO 217, Hq AAF Sta 112, dd 4 Aug 44, are fur asgd, eff 4 Aug 44, to orgns indicated:

```
CREW AF-51 (FP900BA/16305BA-33/33)      TO: 533rd Bomb Sq (H)
2D LT EDWARD C. CARR   01080093 AC (P)  2D LT ELLIS E. RICHARD 0714568 AC (CP)
2D LT EUGENE L. NELSON 0723149 AC (N)   2D LT HUGH W. TREADWELL 0708027 AC (B)
Sgt(757)Albert D. Hines    35608948     Sgt(748)Rudolph S. Staszko 37469124
Cpl(611)William J. Collins 33600428     Cpl(611)Glenn L. Lamp     15174303
Cpl(611)David A. Phillips  31399137     Cpl(611)Robert W. Whitaker 35697441

CREW AF-53 (FB333CJ/16209CJ-187/187)    TO: 533rd Bomb Sq (H)
2D LT ROBERT J. GOTTHARDT 0765248 AC (P) 2D LT RODNEY M. LAYTON   0824145 AC (CP)
2D LT EDGAR G. SCOOMES 0718434 AC (N)   2D LT ROBERT O. STEPHENS 0769226 AC (B)
Cpl(757)Donald J. Ellingham 36657893    Sgt(748)Howard M. Norman  17065516
Cpl(611)Edward B. Bailey   35875498     Cpl(611)David T. Baird    37501610
Cpl(611)Richard A. Bishop  35228764     Pfc(611)Leonard L. Fahnestock 33544109

CREW AF-54 (FB333CJ/16209CJ-240/240)    TO: 534th Bomb Sq (H)
2D LT OMAR P. FULTON   0820989 AC (P)   2D LT ROBERT B. HARRINGTON 0765537 AC(CP)
2D LT ROBERT X. CONLY  0723293 AC (N)
Pvt(757)Roger A. Martin    36598127     Sgt(612)Franklin S. Berry  37154192
Sgt(611)Charles W. Hill    16072941     Sgt(748)Theodore L. Jefferson 19124659
Sgt(611)Carl J.Von Goeben, Jr 20241492  Pvt(611)James C. Grubbs    35583739

CREW AF-55 (FB333CJ/16209CJ-227/227)    TO: 534th Bomb Sq (H)
2D LT ROBERT P. SCHOLZE 0555452 AC (P)  F/O GORDON G. GREGOIRE  T61988 AC (CP)
2D LT JAMES R. FOSTER  0717543 AC (N)   2D LT JAMES M. McGILVRAY 0769337 AC (B)
Cpl(757)Marion M. Freestone 17152381    Sgt(748)Dorin A. Bonham   18084318
Sgt(748)Robert D. Pettus   6251522      Cpl(612)Gale H. Kay, Jr   17056028
Cpl(611)Glen C. Pomeranke  37571226     Cpl(611)Leo J. Schnitker  37476470

CREW AF-58 (FB333CJ/16209CJ-230/230)    TO: 535th Bomb Sq (H)
2D LT RICHARD A. MITCHELL 0555306 AC(P) F/O RAY. BOONE   T62312 AC (CP)
2D LT JAMES F. ARNOLD  0723265 AC (N)   2D LT FRED H. AVERY   0708063 AC (B)
Sgt(757)William J. Trainor 15171246     Sgt(748)Leo J. Dungan, Jr 38406030
Sgt(612)Howard A. Hermel   37565345     Sgt(748)Harold P. Macklin 37526140
Sgt(611)Clarence C. Sapienza 36475065   Cpl(611)Glenn W. Hall     35807165
```

2. So much of par 3, SO 172, this Hq, cs, pert to EM, TD, Clacton-on-the-Sea, as reads: "and again on 29 Jul 44", is amended to read: "and again on 5 Aug 44".

3. Sgt (860) Nassam Abraham 33188781, 535th Bomb Sq (H), is placed on TD for twenty-seven(27)days with 13th Spec Sv Co, AAF Sta 101, eff 6 Aug 44, to proceed to such places in UK necessary to carry out orders of CG. RTR w/o delay to ARC Sv Club, Norwich, to rpt prior to 1800 hrs, 6 Aug 44. Mon alws atzd in accordance with provisions of Reg 30-3, Hq USSTAF, 29 Jan 44, where govt rat and qrs are not furn while traveling and while on TD. CERS. TCNT, under auth ltr Hq ETOUSA 24 May 44. TDN. 60-136 F 432-02 A 0425-24. Auth: TT, 1 BD, #A-214-C.

By order of Colonel LEBER:

```
                                              KARL B. GREENLEE
                                              Major, Air Corps
                                              Adjutant
OFFICIAL:   Karl B. Greenlee
            KARL B. GREENLEE
            Major, Air Corps
            Adjutant

                      RESTRICTED
```

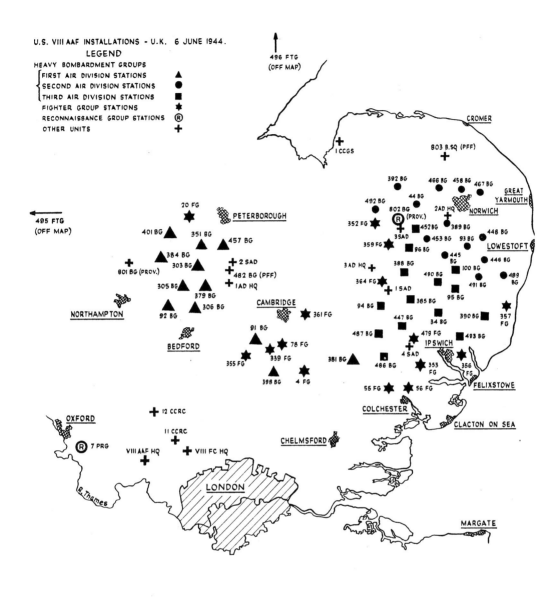

Eighth Air Force Stations in England, 1944

From the Roger A. Freeman book
"The Mighty Eighth"

The Crew
Front L/R: Bob Whitaker, Bill Collins, Ellis Richard,
Dave Phillips. Rear L/R: Al Hines, Hugh Treadwell, Rudy Staszko,
Gene Nelson, Ed Carr

London
Ed Carr, Gene Nelson, friend

533 BS planes over England.
B-17 No. 025 <u>Dreambaby</u> in foreground and No. 570(W) <u>Lucky Me</u> in background. Army Air Force photographer.

B-17's of the 533 BS planes over fields of East Anglica.
No. 503 X <u>Princess Pat</u> in foreground and No. 791 (V) in background.
Army Air Force photographer.

Ridgewell 1944
L-R: Ed Carr, Hugh Treadwell, Ellis Richard, Bob Whitaker (sitting), Al Hines,
Rudy Staszko, Bill Collins

L-R: Ed Carr, Ellis Richard, Dave Phillips, Al Hines,
Bill Collins, Rudy Staszko

Ridgewell 1944
Dave Phillips and Al Hines

Spetchley Park R&R
Center 1944.
Dave Phillips, Bill Collins, Al Hines.
Kneeling: Bob Whitaker,
Rudy Staszko

Local flight from Ridgewell 1944.
L-R: Two unknown airmen, Ed Carr, Ellis Richard,
Gene Nelson

S-Sgt. Phillips Wins Fifth Oak Leaf Cluster

For "meritorious achievement" in aerial combat, S/Sgt. David A. Phillips, USAAF, son of Mr. and Mrs. Joseph K. Phillips of Tenney hill, Kittery Point, has been awarded a fifth oak leaf cluster to his air medal at an Eighth air force bomber station in England.

Sergeant Phillips, a B17 Flying Fortress ball turret gunner, has taken part in 35 bombing attacks on German targets. He is serving with the 381 bombardment group commanded by Lt. Col. Conway S. Hall of North Little Rock, Ark.

He won his wings upon graduation from aerial gunnery school at Tyndall field, Fla., in March, 1944. After completing combat phase training with a bomber crew at Dyersburg, Tenn., he went overseas in July, 1944, to join his squadron.

Sergeant Phillips was graduated from Traip academy in 1943. Before entering the army air force Oct. 5, 1944, he was employed as a clerk for Frisbee Brothers grocery. He has one brother, Joseph K. Phillips, Jr., carpenter's mate 3/c, USNR, stationed in the South Pacific.

SGT. PAUL E. MARSTON, USAAF, camera repairman (left), and Sgt. David A. Phillips, USAAF, air crew ball turret gunner, both residents of Kittery, take time out at an eighth air force bomber station in England to talk over news from home. Groundman Marston formerly was a news photographer for the Portsmouth Herald

---

THIS LICENCE EXPIRES ON THE 31st JULY NEXT.   2

GUN LICENCE 10s.   HW 003329

† MR. PHILLIPS David A.

of A.P.O 557.   in the

Civil Parish or Township of Ridgewell air base within the

Administrative County* of Essex

is hereby authorized to CARRY AND USE A GUN in Great Britain and Northern Ireland from the date hereof until and including the *Thirty-first day of July* next following: the sum of TEN SHILLINGS having been paid for this Licence.

Granted at Ridgewell at 3 hours 18 minutes p.m.

o'clock this 4th day of November 1944

by Roads.

NOTICE.—1. This Licence will not authorize any person to purchase, have in his possession, use, or carry any firearms (as defined in the Firearms Act, 1937) in respect of which it is necessary to hold a firearm Certificate granted under the said Act unless he holds such Certificate.

2. Any permanent change of address should be notified to the County or County Borough Council in whose area the Licensee's former address is situate.

†Insert full Christian Names and Surname IN BLOCK LETTERS.
*If the residence is within a County Borough, strike out "Administrative" and insert "Borough" after "County".

Ridgewell Church

The Warren, Daves Ridgewell Friends

Dave at Warren's Cottage

Ridgewell Main Gate
Christmas 1944

Riding to hounds near Spetchley Park Rand R

Spetchley Park Rand R near Worcester

Lt. Bob Gotthardt
Rapid City, S.D.
1944

Lt. Bob Gotthardt
with 381st Bomb Group in
Ridgewell, 1944

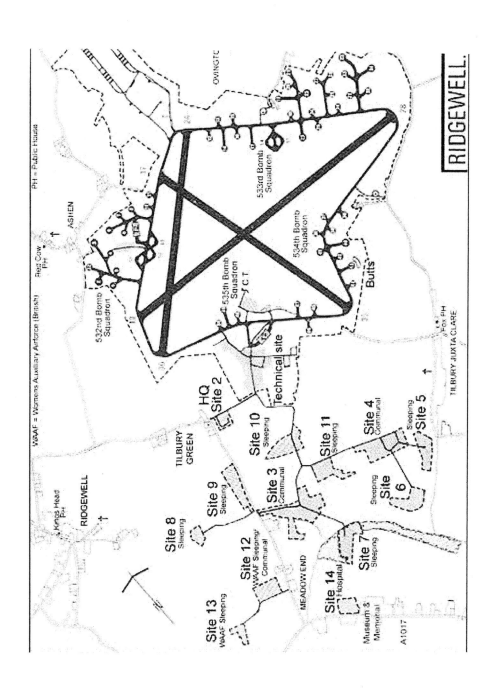

Map of Ridgewell Airbase and surrounding area

157

HEADQUARTERS EIGHTH AIR FORCE
Office of the Commanding General

8 Nov 44

SPECIAL ORDERS)
NUMBER...305)

E X T R A C T

*   *   *

8. The following O, AC, are DP, temp promoted to the gr indicated in AUS w/rank fr date of this order. (Auth Cir 90, Hq European T of Opns USA, 17 August 1944):

*   *   *

2nd Lt to 1st Lt

*   *   *

EDWARD C. CARR, 01080093
JOHN D. EVANS, 0772035
ROBERT T. HILMES, 0717654

ROBERT J. ROUSH, 0564182
FRED (NMI) HOLLENDORFER, 0821020
BURTON H. KINNEY, 0814498
SAMUEL J. REISMAN, 0772731

EDGAR G. SCOONES, 0718434

*   *   *

By command of Lieutenant General DOOLITTLE:

JOHN S. ALLARD
Brigadier General, USA,
Chief of Staff

OFFICIAL:

/s/ Lindsey L. Braxton
/t/ LINDSEY L. BRAXTON
Colonel, AGD,
Adjutant General

A TRUE EXTRACT COPY:

Charles R. McCarthy
CHARLES R. McCARTHY
Captain, Air Corps
Personnel Officer

An early mission of the 381st Bomb Group

381st B-17's on flight line at Ridgewell

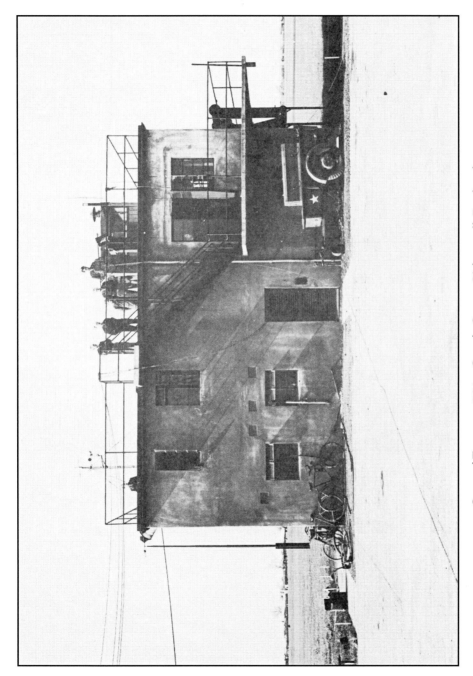

Control Tower at 381st Bomb Group, Ridgewell, England

381st Plane at "Bombs Away"

Going through flak on a bomb run

Photos from the ball turret
by Dave Phillips

London Leave
Ed Carr, Hugh Treadwell, Gene Nelson

Targets — before and after

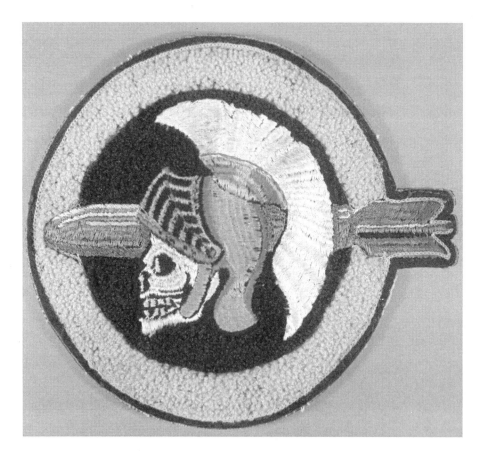

533rd Bomb Squadron patch

MEMORANDUM MEMORANDUM

LT. E.L. NELSON 0-723149
DY 6-30
CREW # 198-51
K.A.A.F.
KEARNEY, NEBRASKA
JULY 1, 1944

LT. EUGENE L. NELSON 0-723149
% COMMANDANT OF CREWS
Box 1189
D.A.A.F.
DYERSBURG, TENN.
MAY 14, 1944

MEMORANDUM MEMORANDUM

GOOSE BAY, LABRADOR
JULY 12, 1944 — — —
MEEK'S FIELD
KEFLAVIK, ICELAND
JULY 13, 1944

GRENNIER FIELD
MANCHESTER, N.H.
JULY 10, 1944

Gene Nelson's diary, July 1944 to March 1945

STATION # 112
BOVINGDON, ENGLAND
JULY 23, 1944

STATION # 167 APO 557
381ST BOMB GT. 533B.SQD.
RIDGEWELL, ENG.
AUG. 5, 1944

A.T.C.
VALLEY, WALES U.K.
JULY 15, 1944

— REPLACEMENT POOL
STONE, ENGLAND
JULY 16, 1944

1945

MEMORANDUM

FEB. 6 - #27 - WEIMAR, GER.
TGT. OF OPPORTUNITY. I FLEW
AS GP. LEAD NAVIGATOR + D.R'D
MYSELF ALL OVER GERMANY'S
FLAK INSTALLATIONS - ALL NAV.
AIDS OUT - WEATHER BAD ON
RETURN - CEILING 300'. I SURE
SWEATED THIS ONE OUT
FEB. 19 - #28 - DORTMUND -
SYNTHETIC OIL PLANT - GROUP
LEAD, GEE-H - MODERATE
INACCURATE FLAK - NICE MISSION
FEB. 25 - #29 - MUNICH - VISUAL -
VERY ACCURATE FLAK - OUR
SHIP WAS HIT HARD - TODAY,
I SAW LAKE CONSTANCE + THE
ALPS - VERY BEAUTIFUL SCENERY -
EXCELLENT RESULTS -
MAR. 10 - #30 - THE LAST ONE -
DORTMUND - A FINE MISSION
EXCEPT THAT I LOST ALL
OF MY NAVIGATIONAL AIDS -
G + MICKEY BOTH WENT OUT -
BOTH BOY I'M ALL DONE -

MEMORANDUM

AUG. 13 - MISSION # 1
ROUEN, FRANCE -
TARGET - ROAD JUNCTION -
FLAK EXTREMELY ACCURATE -
SHIP HIT IN NOSE + TAIL
AUG. 14 - #2 METZ, FRANCE
S. ENG. AIRFIELD - NO FLAK -
" MILK RUN "
AUG. 26 - #3 - GELSENKIRCHEN,
GER. (HAPPY VALLEY)
SYNTHETIC OIL REFINERY -
BARRAGE FLAK - HEAVIEST
FLAK EVER SEEN - SHIP HIT
IN WINGS AND FUSELAGE -
AUG. 30 #4 - KIEL - BOAT PENS -
HEAVY FLAK - SHIP HIT IN NOSE,
WINGS, AND ONE ENGINE OUT.
ROUGH MISSION - 7 HRS.

Gene Nelson's diary, July 1944 to March 1945

MEMORANDUM

SEPT. 3 - #5 - LUDWIGSHAVEN
CHEMICAL WORKS - 35 MIN.
BOMB RUN - HEAVY FLAK
FROM I.P. TO TARGET - 9 HRS.

SEPT. 9 - #6 - LUDWIGSHAVEN -
HEAVY FLAK - ACCURATE - SHIP
SHOT ALL TO HELL - ROUGHEST
MISSION YET

SEPT. 11 - #7 - MERESBURG -
HEAVY FLAK - ME-109'S ATTACKED
REAR OF FORMATION - NO DAMAGE

SEPT. 17 - # 8 - EINHOVEN
GROUND SUPPORT - BEAUTIFUL
MISSION - NO FLAK - NO FIGHTERS
INVASION OF HOLLAND
SEPT. 19 - #9 HAMM, GERMANY -
MARSHALLING YARDS & R.R. BRIDGE
FLAK VERY ACCURATE - WEATHER
POOR - SNOWSTORM OVER TARGET
SEPT. 25, #10 - FRANKFURT
MARSHALLING YARDS - HEAVY
FLAK, BUT INACCURATE -
SQUADRON LEAD

MEMORANDUM

SEPT. 26 #11 - OSNABRUCK -
1ST. WING LEAD - MARSHALLING YARDS
LIGHT FLAK -

OCT. 2 - #12 - SQD. LEAD - KASSEL
LIGHT ACCURATE FLAK OVER TARGET -
HEAVY FLAK DURING "SIGHTSEEING
TOUR" OF HAPPY VALLEY

OCT. 5 - #13 - DEPUTY LEAD - COLOGNE
GERMANY - HEAVY FLAK - PFF.

OCT. 17 - #14 - SQD. LEAD - COLOGNE
PFF - SHIP HIT IN NOSE - ABOUT AN
8" HOLE - I THOUGHT I HAD IT -
2 J.P.'S SEEN
OCT. 25 #15 - GROUP LEAD - HAMBURG
PFF - BEAUTIFUL MISSION - INTENSE
FLAK BUT INACCURATE -
OCT. 30 - NO MISSION, BUT A DAY I'LL
NEVER FORGET
NOV. 4 - #16 - GROUP LEAD - WITH LEBER
HAMBURG - INACCURATE FLAK
NOV. 26 #17. GR. LD. WITH COL LEBER - R.R.
VIADUCT AT ALTENBEKEN - NO FLAK
BUT LUFTWAFFE WAS UP IN FORCE -
GR. AHEAD OF US & BEHIND US HIT
BY ME-109'S & FW-190'S - 2 PASSES AT 16C

−55°C   MEMORANDUM

DEC. 9 - #18 - STUTTGART, GER.
LONG MISSION - MODERATE FLAK
BUT VERY ACCURATE - GROUP LEAD

DEC. 18 - #19 - COLOGNE, GER.
WING LEAD - ALTITUDE 31,250 FT.
TEMP. -50°C - GOOD MISSION -
LIGHT INACCURATE FLAK - SIX
WIND SHIFTS AT ALTITUDE -
DENSE PERSISTENT CON-TRAILS

DEC. 24 - #20 - TWAS THE DAY
BEFORE X-MAS AND THE
381st. WENT TO AN AIRFIELD
NORTH OF FRANKFURT -
VISUAL TGT. AND RESULTS
WERE EXCELLENT

DEC. 31 - #21 - PRUM, GER.
R.R. MARSHALLING YARDS - DIRECT
SUPPORT TO GROUND TROOPS -
WE WERE IN ENEMY TERRITORY
FOR 20 MINUTES. NO FLAK EITHER
JAN. 1, 1945 - #22 - MAGDEBURG, GER
"FIGHTER SWEEP" - BANDITS HIT
FORMATION BEHIND US - A ROUGH
MISSION - TOO MUCH FLAK & FIGHTERS

MEMORANDUM

JAN. 6, 1945 #23 - COLOGNE - R.R. BRIDGE
LIGHT FLAK - VERY UNEVENTFUL -

JAN. 14 - #24 - COLOGNE, AUTO-
BAHN BRIDGE OVER RHINE.
TARGET KNOCKED OUT -
FLAK MOST ACCURATE I
HAVE EVER SEEN - I WAS
HIT IN THE FOREHEAD AND
IN THE ARM - (NOT A PURPLE
HEART CASE THOUGH)

JAN. 29 - #25 - COBLENZ -
R.R. MARSHALLING YARDS - NKE
MISSION - LIGHT FLAK & VERY
INACCURATE

FEB. 3 - #26 - THIS WAS IT - BIG "B"
BERLIN - VISUAL TGT. - WE WERE THE
LAST GR TO HIT AND BY THAT TIME
THE CITY WAS FLAMING AND SMOKE
ROSE UP TO 10,000 FT. FLAK WAS
MODERATE BUT VERY ACCURATE.
WE LOST TWO SHIPS OVER THE TGT.

Gene Nelson's diary, July 1944 to March 1945

169

Gene Nelson – One Pound Note – Short Snorter

STATIONS : 0945
START ENG: 1000
TAXI : 1015
TAKE-OFF : 1030
LV FLD : 1144
ALTITUDE : 13,500'
LAST T/O : 1130

200th MISSION

9 OCTOBER 1944

38/1st

SPARES:
PFF: - 036
Lead: 4A -7852
2Q - 8497
40 - 0011

. . . .
Lead Squadron, "C" Group, 1st Combat Bomb Wing   532nd

MacNEILL - GUY
PFF 2E 8010
NASHOLD   MILLER
2N 7675   PFF 2F 7990

SCHOMBURG   LANG
2M 2703   "B"   "C"   5P 7265
BENDALL   MARSHALL   GARRETT   BOWMAN
2C 7536   2D 7100   5X 7267   5Y 7553
REED
2H 2873
COPELAND   SEELEY
2B 8103   2P 1575

. . . .
High Squadron, "C" Group   534th

KAURIN - FORD
PFF 5I 7625
PJORNESS   MOORE
4C 7285   4H 6173

EVANS   STUART
4N 2968   "B"   5Z 7538
WILKINSON   BLACK   SMITH   ROJOHN
4B 7514   4F 2966   5R 1990   4M 8114
PARKISON   CLARK
4Q 6115   4J 8159
SCHILLING   SCHOLZE
4I 7657   4G 1550

. . . .
Low Squadron, "C" Group   533rd

MASTERSON - JONES
4D 8158
WINSOR   ROUSH
3X 7503   3K 7882

GOTTHARDT   JARVILL
3V 7791   "B"   5M 2590
GARDNER   CARR   LEVITOFF   THORNTON
3T 9997   3P 2025   2A 8550   4K 7076
HUBER
30 1761
KINNEY   LONG
2L 7969   3W 6478

171

The crew that crash-landed in Belgium on 10 Jan 45 with Hugh Treadwell aboard signed a piece of fabric from the damaged tail section of the plane.

(Courtesy of Stuart Newman)

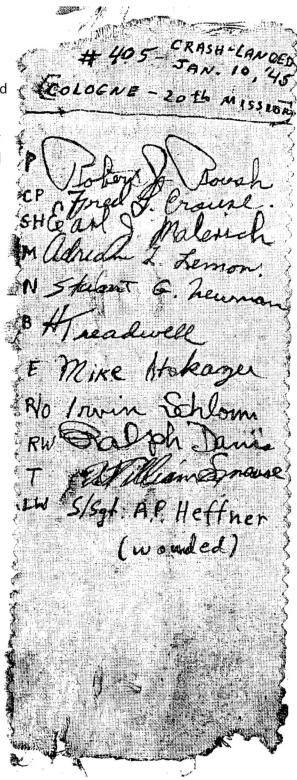

Hugh Treadwell was bombardier on B-17 on loan from 303rd BG, hit by flak over Cologne and landed near Ghent, Belgium, 10 January 1945. Photos courtesy of Mike Malerich, son of Earl Malerich.

January 10, 1945
<u>1st Row – Left to Right</u>
2nd Lt. Adrian L. Lemon (P.F.F. Navigator)
1st Lt. Robert J. Roush (Pilot)
2nd Lt. Fred L. Crouse (Co-Pilot)
2nd Lt. Stuart G. Newman (D.R. navigator)

<u>2nd Row – Left to Right</u>
T/Sgt. Irvin Schlom (Radio Operator)
S/Sgt. Richard E. Davis (Rt. Waist Gunner)
S/Sgt. William "Pete" C. Sprouse (Tail Gunner)
1st Lt. Earl J. Malerich, Jr. (GeeH Navigator)
Sgt. Michael Stohazu (Eng. & Top Turret Gunner)

<u>Missing from picture</u>
1st Lt. Hugh W. Treadwell (Bombardier) – taking picture
S/Sgt. Arthur C. Hafner (Lt. Waist Gunner) – taken to
medical facility, amputated right leg below knee.

Photo courtesy of Mike Malerich, son of Earl Malerich.

Ed Carr's Mission check-off calendar
1944 – 1945

16 February 1945

CERTIFICATE OF OPERATIONAL MISSIONS

NAME Edward C. Carr   RANK 1st Lt ASN O-1080093   POSTION Pilot

COMBAT HOURS 269:10

DATE	TARGET
13 Aug 44	Gace, France
14 Aug 44	Metz, France
26 Aug 44	Gelsenkirchen, Germany
30 Aug 44	Kiel, Germany
3 Sep 44	Ludwigshaven, Germany
9 Sep 44	Ludwigshaven, Germany
11 Sep 44	Merseburg, Germany
17 Sep 44	Eindhoven, Holland
19 Sep 44	Hamm, Germany
25 Sep 44	Frankfurt, Germany
27 Sep 44	Cologne, Germany
28 Sep 44	Magdeburg, Germany
9 Oct 44	Schweinfurt, Germany
14 Oct 44	Cologne, Germany
17 Oct 44	Cologne, Germany
25 Oct 44	Hamburg, Germany
28 Oct 44	Munster, Germany
9 Nov 44	Metz, Germany
10 Nov 44	Cologne, Germany
21 Nov 44	Merseburg, Germany
25 Nov 44	Merseburg, Germany
29 Nov 44	Misburg, Germany
11 Dec 44	Ludwigshaven, Germany
24 Dec 44	Kirch Gons, Germany
31 Dec 44	Prum, Germany
1 Jan 45	Kassel, Germany
5 Jan 45	Heimbach, Germany
3 Jan 45	Cologne, Germany
6 Jan 45	Cologne, Germany
10 Jan 45	Ostheim, Germany
14 Jan 45	Rodenkirchen, Germany
20 Jan 45	Mannheim, Germany
29 Jan 45	Niederlahnstein, Germany
1 Feb 45	Mannheim, Germany
14 Feb 45	Brux, Czech.

-1-

"CERTIFIED CORRECT"

William F. Carpenter
WILLIAM F. CARPENTER,
Capt., Air Corps,
Operations Officer.
533rd Bomb Sq (H)

WAR DEPARTMENT
THE ADJUTANT GENERAL'S OFFICE
WASHINGTON 25, D. C.

AGPD-R 201 Carr, Edward C.
(24 Jul 45) O 1080093

3 November 1945

SUBJECT: Distinguished Flying Cross

TO: First Lieutenant Edward C. Carr
1800 Austin Street
Waco, Texas

1. Reference is made to your letter dated 24 July 1945, concerning the award of the Distinguished Flying Cross.

2. By direction of the President, you have been awarded the Distinguished Flying Cross by the Commanding General, First Air Division. The citation is as follows:

DISTINGUISHED FLYING CROSS

"For extraordinary achievement while serving as Pilot of a B-17 airplane on bombing missions over Germany and enemy occupied Europe, 10 November 1944, 21 November 1944, 10 January 1945 and 14 February 1945. The outstanding flying ability and exemplary initiative evinced by Lieutenant Carr on these operations contributed materially to their successful completion. In the face of numerous hazards and difficulties, the calm resolution of this officer was instrumental in the safe return of aircraft and crew to home base despite severe damage sustained by the airplane. Demonstrating exceptional airmanship on other occasions, Lieutenant Carr assumed the lead of the Squadron when the lead aircraft was forced to abandon formation and dexterously completed the missions. The courage, coolness and skill displayed by this officer reflect the highest credit upon himself and the Armed Forces of the United States."

3. The decoration will be forwarded to the Commanding General, Eighth Service Command, Dallas, Texas, who will select an officer to present the decoration to you. The officer selected will communicate with you concerning your wishes in the matter.

BY ORDER OF THE SECRETARY OF WAR:

ADJUTANT GENERAL

ED CARR 533rd

Date	TARGET	AIRCRAFT	VP-
	With Ellis Richard	July '44	
13/8/44	ROUEN	42-32025 - DREAM BABY	P
14/8	METZ	42-32025 - DREAM BABY	P
26/8	GELSENKIRCHEN	42-32025 - DREAM BABY	P
3/9	LUDWIGSHAFEN	42-32025 - DREAM BABY	P
9/9	MANNHEIM	42-97357 - THE RAILROADER	Z
11/9	MERSEBURG	42-38159 Colonel Bub 534th GD-	J
17/9	EINDHOVEN	42-40007 - HONEY	M
19/9	HAMM	42-40007 - HONEY	M
25/9	FRANKFURT	42-32025 - DREAM BABY	P
28/9	MAGDEBURG	42-32025 - DREAM BABY	P
9/10	SCHWEINFURT	42-32025 - DREAM BABY	P
17/10	COLOGNE	42-39997 - BIG MIKE/FRENCHY'S FOLLY	T
25/10	HAMBURG	42-97589	Y
30/10	MUNSTER	42-97059 - MARSHA SUE	S
9/11	HAMBURG	42-97589	Y
10/11	COLOGNE	42-97589	Y
21/11	MERSEBURG	42-97589	Y
25/11	MERSEBURG	42-39997 - BIG MIKE/FRENCHY'S FOLLY	T
26/11	ALTENBEKEN	42-32025 - DREAM BABY	P
11/12	MANNHEIM	42-97313 - COLUMBUS MISS 5th MS-N	
24/12	ETTINGHAUSEN	42-97589	Y
31/12	PRUM	42-97589	Y
	No January or 1st half feb lists		
14/2/45	BRUX	44-8983 FORT LANSING EMANCIPATOR	S
19/2	Completed Tour - Sent to 70th RD - DFC 12/3/45		

Aircraft Flown on 23 of 35 missions

(Information from Dave Osborne 1986-Kingshead, Ridgewell)

HEADQUARTERS
381ST BOMBARDMENT GROUP (H) AAF
Office of the Group Commander
APO 557

201-Carr, Edward C.   14 February 1945

SUBJECT: Combat Experience.

TO   : Whom It May Concern.

1. This is to certify that Edward C. Carr, O-1080093,
1st Lt., Air Corps, arrived in the European Theater of Operations
on 12 July 1944 and has completed his operational tour of duty as
a member of a combat crew on a B-17 aircraft.

2. The record of his combat experience is as follows:

   a. Combat Crew Position: Pilot
   b. Number of Operational Missions: Thirty-five
   c. Date of last mission: 14 February 1945
   d. Number of enemy aircraft destroyed: None
   e. Decorations awarded: Air Medal with five Oak
      Leaf Clusters
   f. Manner of performance of duty: Excellent

3. It is recommended that he be reassigned to further combat
in another theater after a period of rest in the Zone of Interior.

RECEIVED
17 FEB 1945
HQ. 1st COMBAT
BOMB WING

                                    CONWAY S. HALL,
                                    Lt. Colonel, Air Corps,
                                    Commanding.

                          1st Ind.
HQ. 1st Combat Bombardment Wing (H), APO 557, 16 February 1945.

TO: Whom It May Concern.

   Approved.

                                    WILLIAM M. GROSS,
                                    Brigadier General, USA,
                                    Commanding.

                          -1-

179

SPECIAL ORDERS)   HQ 1ST AIR DIVISION
NO.   46)   APO 557. 15 February 1945
                           E X T R A C T

1. Under the provisions of Sec III, WD Cir 372, 13 Sep 44 and 8AF Memo 35-1, 22 Sep
44, fol named O and EM are reld fr dy and asgmt orgns indicated; are reasgd and/or
trfd in gr to Cas Pool 70th Repl Depot Sta 591. Pers will rpt on earliest practicable
date subsequent to presentation of all DFC and AM awarded (and/or recommended or in
process of being recommended) pers to be retained not in excess of ten (10) days) to
await ret to ZI. O and EM will have clothing and equip listed in Sec I, Cir 110, Hq
European T of Opns USA,12 Nov 44, as amended by Sec III, Cir 125, same hq, 27 Dec
44, before leaving present sta. Reimbursement for qrs not to exceed $4.00 per day and
$1.25 per day for subs is auth these O while in travel status to Sta 591; FD will
reimburse EM alws prescribed in Cir 63, Hq European T of Opns USA, 5 Jun 44 as amended
by Sec IX Cir 84, same hq, 31 Jul 44, if qrs and/or rat are not avail while in travel
status to Sta 591. This is a perm change of sta. WPR and/or GMV. TWA. TCNT 60-136
P 431-02 A 212/50425. TDN.

36th Bomb Squadron

CAPT LLOYD S. RICKS O446753 AC(P)   T/Sgt (538) Ernest O. Asseln 37462657

91st Bomb Group

1ST LT ANTHONY W. THEIS 0714827 AC(P)   S/Sgt (611) Clayton W. Hahn 17088914
                                         S/Sgt (748) Richard H. Hayes 33647180

92nd Bomb Group

1ST LT HERBERT A. GRAY JR 02056580 AC(N)   1ST LT THOMAS P. MEDLEY 01997878 AC(N)
1ST LT OTTAVIO V. PEZZI 0824203 AC(P)   1ST LT DELMA O. BEARD 0767463 AC(P)
1ST LT JAMES A. SMITH 0764575 AC(P)   1ST LT LEO V. GEIGER 0765647 AC(B)
1ST LT WALTER E. WOODROW 0771198 AC(P)   1ST LT HERSCHEL CROWLEY JR 0717629 AC(N)
1ST LT IRA J. HECHLER 02056589 AC(N)   T/Sgt (748) John (NMI) Malak 16111791
T/Sgt (748) Loyce W. Whatley 38245107   T/Sgt (748) Warren L. Frederick 32883448
T/Sgt (748) Robert W. Butz 13157965   S/Sgt (612) Alexander J. Anderson/
S/Sgt (612) Finnell Hansen 39417064   35765377
S/Sgt (612) Earl G. Popp 36330025   S/SGT (611) James R. Sauer 35879607
T/Sgt (757) Fred C. Van Buren 37478378   T/Sgt (748) James B. Bruce 34651363
S/Sgt (612) John M. Boggs 35773259   S/Sgt (612) Edward V. Makloski 19124601
S/Sgt (612) James J. McCoy 16187977

303rd Bomb Group

1ST LT MARVIN H. HECKENDORF 0770657 AC(P)   1ST LT ARTHUR B. MIDDLEMAS 0771484 AC(P)
2ND LT ROY P. MALONE 02C00306 AC(N)   T/Sgt (748) Hubert W. Gallman 14070182
S/Sgt (611) Robert L. Barris 35068146   S/Sgt (612) Ralph V. Evans 37721024
S/Sgt (612) Raymond W. Lary 36839512

305th Bomb Group

1ST LT THEODORE A. POREBSKI 0768656 AC(P)   2ND LT PHILIP D. KJELMYR 0761966 AC(P)
T/Sgt (748) Robert D. Erwin 37477853   T/Sgt (757) Rudolph J. Bryan 13128833
S/Sgt (612) Thomas H. Roy 18210002   S/Sgt (612) Lowrie G. Simms 36694417
S/Sgt (612) Leon R. Wilson 38507039
2ND LT CARL D. COOPER 0770958 AC(P)

306th Bomb Group

1ST LT CARL B. HATHAWAY 0766385 AC(P)   1ST LT WALTER M. LANIUS JR 0558721 AC(N)
T/Sgt (748) Bernard F. Munnerlyn 18168231   T/Sgt (612) Barney Parker Jr 34796102
S/Sgt (612) John C. Kieffer 37726752   S/Sgt (612) Russell H. Schuettpelz/
                                                                   36836162

351st Bomb Group

T/Sgt (757) Earl F. McCracken Jr 16150644   T/Sgt (757) Richard T. Patton 15126615

381st Bomb Group

1ST LT ARTHUR S. CARTER JR 0557874 AC(B)   1ST LT EDWARD C. CARR 01080093 AC(P)
1ST LT JOHN A. CONKLIN JR 0722283 AC(N)   1ST LT DONOVAN L. CHAMBERLIN 0767743 AC(P)
1ST LT JAMES (NMI) SCOTT 0710328 AC(N)   S/Sgt (611) Robert W. Winter 31355061

398th Bomb Group

S/Sgt (612) Wilbert F. Kendall 36860916   1ST LT ERNEST O. ANDREWS 0766983 AC(P)
1ST LT RALPH H. MCINTYRE 0712456 AC(N)   S/Sgt (748) Robert E. Pruner 38394122
Cpl (612) Thomas E. Dougherty 16123094   S/Sgt (612) Charlie M. Carter 14067131
S/Sgt (612) Arnold W. Hoffman 32465264   S/Sgt (612) John W. Hunter 15975778
T/Sgt (748) Sidney K. Trigher 19161586

401st Bomb Group

T/Sgt (748) Robert L. Jencks 39201625   T/Sgt (757) Samuel T. Richardson 19084615
T/Sgt (748) Emmitt E. Warren 18162393
S/Sgt (612) George Importe 39138837
Baggage will accompany pers upon change of sta. US Strategic Air Forces in Europe

(SO # 46 Hq 1AD 15 Feb 45 contd)

1. (contd)
Reg No. 80-10, as amended, 5 Aug 44, will be complied with. S/Rs and allied papers will accompany EM upon change of sta. Sta Comdr will insure that ea O and EM has at least two (2) copies of the SO immediately avail on arrival at new sta.

*   *   *   *   *

By command of Brigadier General TURNER:

BARTLETT BEAMAN
Brigadier General, USA
Chief of Staff

OFFICIAL:

ROBERTS F. JOHNSON, JR.
Lieut Colonel, AGD
Adjutant General

DISTRIBUTION: "B"

WAR DEPARTMENT
AIR CORPS FORM No. 104A
APPROVED JULY 28, 1937

SHIPPING TICKET

PREPARED BY

CONSIGNOR EDWARD C. CARR 1st Lt AC
0-108093

CONSIGNEE 533rd Bomb Sq(H) 381st Bomb Gp (H)
AAF Stat 167 APO 557

ACCOUNTABILITY

DATE 17 Feb 1945

SHIPPING OFFICER'S VOUCHER NO.

SHIPPING ORDER : CLASS   NO.   PAGE

DATE SHIPPED

SHIP BY   SELECTED BY

INSPECTED BY   PACKED BY

AUTH. OR REF. NO. FLYING CLOTHING
B/L NO.   ROUTING

STOCK LOCATION	QUANTITY ORDERED	UNIT	NAME CHANGED TO	TYPE PART NO.	NAME	UNIT COST	TOTAL COST
	1	ea	Jacket winter	B-11			
	1	ea	Jacket interm	A-10			
	1	ea	Trousers winter	A-10			
	1	ea	Trousers interm.	A9			
	1	ea	Suit summer	AN531			
	1	pr	Shoes winter	A6			
	1	pr	Gloves winter	A11			
	1	pr	Gloves rayon	insert			
	1	pr	Gloves summer	B3			
	1	ea	Helmet winter	A11			
	1	ea	Helmet summer	AN15			
	1	ea	Mask oxygen	A14			
	1	ea	Goggles assy	B8			
	1	ea	Glasses sun	AN			
	1	ea	Watch hack	A11			
	1	ea	Flashlight	TL122b			
			LAST ITEM				

COPY-201 File

CERTIFICATE

I certify that the items listed hereon were turned in to me by the above named individual and that the individual does not possess a Form 121 or have any equipment records in his 201 file.

G. N. CRYMES
1st Lt AC

THIS COPY TO

RECEIVED
NAME AND RANK
SIGNATURE

DATE
RECEIVING OFFICER'S VOUCHER NO.
POSTED TO STOCK RECORD BY
HQ.808. 24/2/44 1000M. 22518 Ho. (327)

APO NO.____

C/o POSTMASTER, NEW YORK, NEW YORK

_2 - 19 - 45_
_____
(Date)

CLOTHING AND EQUIPMENT ADJUSTMENT FORM (List of clothing and equipment)

The items listed herein constitute all of the Government clothing and individual equipment in the possession of _Edward Carr_ _O-1080093_ , upon departure from this command. All other items of clothing and equipment have been withdrawn and returned to stock or otherwise disposed of in accordance with regulations. Adjustment of clothing and equipment account is made pursuant to Circular No. 200, War Department, 1944.

Edward Carr / 2*t AC O-1080093
Name, Rank, Serial Number and Orgn.

Gail S. Brewer
(Supply Officer)
GAIL S. BREWER
1st Lt Air Corps
Supply Officer
533rd Bmb Sqd

1 ea Mask, gas, service
1 ea Ointment, protective
1 ea Impregnite, shoe
2 ea Eyeshields, anti-gas
1 ea Bag, canvas, field W/strap
1 ea Cup, canteen
1 ea Spoon
1 ea Knife
1 ea Fork
2 ea Blankets, wool od
1 ea Belt, pistol
1 ea Helmet, steel, M1 complete
1 ea Pouch, first aid
1 ea Roll, bedding, waterproof
1 ea Pouch, magazine, double web
2 ea Tags, identification
1 ea Necklace, identification

Government equipment in Ed Carr's possession when departing
Ridgewell, 19 February 1945

182

Farm fields replace runways at Ridgewell

The old perimeter track and last hanger at Ridgewell

Nissen Hut – now farm building
Ridgewell

Part of old base hospital near Memorial at Ridgewell

Kings Head Pub
Ridgewell 1983

Regulars having a pint at the Kings Head
1983

Steve Worth, ex-proprietor of
Kings Head Pub 1983

381st Bomb Group Memorial Monument
near Ridgewell

Stained Glass
Window

Ridgewell Church

from 381st Bomb
Group Intercom

Letter from
RIDGEWELL CONGREGATIONAL CHURCH

Ray Ater,
3102 Marlin Road,
Louisville, KY40220 USA   13 November 1999
Dear Ray,

We write to express the thanks and appreciation of the Officers and Members of this Church for your participation in our Service of Re-Dedication on the opening of our new building on the 23rd October 1999.

Kindly convey to your Memorial Association our gratitude for the further cheque presented in the sum of G B Pounds £564.53 We are confident that the Memorial Window dedicated to the memory of the 381st Bomb Group will provide a lasting tribute to those who gave their lives in the Second World War

We treasure the personal message from James Good Brown and ask you to convey to him our prayer that God may richly bless him

We will be sending to you further photographs as soon as they are to hand Thank you again Ray for traveling those thousands of miles to share in and make our special day

With every good wish,

Yours sincerely

Peter M. Adams   Hon Sec.

11th Century Church at Ashen, near our base at Ridgewell. 381st veterans have contributed to restoration fund.

photo from 381st BG Intercom

Bill Boeing's branding iron.
Tracing and photograph.

"Drive in" or "Fly in"
To Arnold Field and
visit the

VETERANS' MUSEUM
Halls, Tennessee

*"Return to a moment in time when age meant
nothing and freedom meant everything."*

This museum is located on the site of the
former B-17 Training Facility known as
THE DYERSBURG ARMY AIR BASE,
which was operational from 1942 through
1945. The location itself is a rich and
unforgettable piece of history, which is
memorialized each year with a regional
air show the last weekend in August.

**Open to the general public
2 to 5 p.m. on Saturdays and Sundays
(except on Holidays)**

NO ADMISSION FEE

CHILDREN UNDER THE AGE OF 16 MUST

BE ACCOMPANIED BY AN ADULT

*For tours and private appointments for times other than those
scheduled, call 901-836-7448 and leave a telephone number.*

The Veterans' Museum is a facility that offers
complete WWI and WWII exhibits. Displays on Korea,
Vietnam and Desert Storm are under development.

This museum is located on a former WWII B-17
training base that was operational from 1942-1945. It
turned a sleepy southern town into a major city
overnight; after the war, it returned to a sleepy southern
town just as quickly. All that remains is hundreds of
acres of concrete, the Veterans' Museum, and a yearly
warbird air show the last weekend in August.

Pictures and documents from the National
Archives, materials from WWI, II and Korea
including diaries, personal and official letters,
technical publications, and divisional histories,
WWII military vehicles, uniforms, and videos will
excite adults and give the young an opportunity to
look at history personally.

A gift shop includes airplane and military
vehicle models with profits used to benefit the
museum.

A research library and archives provide
materials for students, teachers, historians and the
community at large.

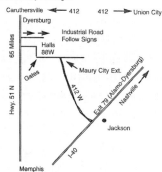

RV Parking Available (Call 901-836-7448 after
9 p.m.) Fly-ins - M31, Runways 36 and 18.

EPILOGUE

"All the Old Familiar Places"

Most WWII veterans that I know have a desire to return to old battlegrounds. Is this because we want to recapture our youth, to briefly experience again exciting days when life was at risk or to rekindle the comradeship of the past? Maybe we want to gain a better understanding of what was happening around us and thus explain the battles in a larger more meaningful context. Also, I think, we want to look for any evidence that might remain of the battle site or a memorial of some kind recording what took place; a place in history.

In the last decade battlefield tours have been big business for the travel industry. Nostalgia sells. There were anniversary tours to the Normandy beaches for D Day, tours to Pearl Harbor, and the East Anglia Tourist Board in 1992 sponsored "Return to England" in honor of the 50th anniversary of the arrival of the Eighth Air Force in England. But the Eighth Air Force fought their battles in the sky high over occupied Europe. There is no plot of ground, a beach, a village that an 8th AF veteran can point to and say, "This is where I fought; this is what we captured." There are no Omaha beaches, Anzios, Tarawas, or Bastognes. There are no monuments marking the places and no plaques explaining the battles that took place five miles in the sky over Germany. The only places of nostalgia that an airman can return to are the air bases he flew from.

In putting together the story of our aircrew I found that photos or mental images of the airbases where we had served helped trigger memories of the crew and of our experiences. The imaging promoted curiosity and a desire to return to the bases where we were stationed and those where I had trained. I wanted to tread the ground again, to find what, if anything, had been done to preserve their history. I had been back to some of the airbases and seeing them again was both a sad and exhilarating experience.

Most WWII Army Air Force bases were located near small towns. They must have had an impact on the local communities. There would have been daily interaction between airmen and civilians. The bases provided employment and an economic boost for the town. To have an airbase near your town was a big deal and people patriotically supported their airbase. Is anyone today keeping an historical record of these WWII AAF bases and of what happened to them after the war? To find out, I could have used Air Force historical records, but I wanted a local flavor, preferring to contact community libraries, museums, and chambers of commerce for my research. I hoped to find out if there was a preserved history of these air bases available to the current generation. The response I received from research librarians, museum docents, and chamber employees was very helpful. I thank them all! The following is the result of my research of the air bases where I trained and where our crew trained or was stationed from Santa Ana, California, to Ridgewell in England.

Training Air Bases

My first days with the Army Air Force were spent at Santa Ana, California. Thinking of that base and what happened to it after the war brings back the words of Simon and Garfunkel, "Where have you gone, Joe DiMaggio?" Joe has gone, but when I was at Santa Ana Pre Flight School in 1943, he was there serving out his military obligation as a physical training instructor. His principal duty, besides playing baseball, was to lead cadet formations in their daily exercise routine. Would having a baseball star lead the troops in "jumping jacks" inspire their performance? Who knows! We do know that the various military branches competed to enroll celebrities for publicity and recruiting purposes. Drafting celebrities also gave validity to the idea of fairness in the Selective Service Program. It wasn't DiMaggio's fault that he did not get more important duties.

Santa Ana Army Air Base was the headquarters for the West Coast Training Command and the site of the Pre Flight School for cadets who would be selected for navigator, bombardier or pilot training. The base was located on 900 acres acquired from the Whittier Estate in 1941, the nearest town being Santa Ana. About 150,000 cadets went through Pre Flight School at SAAAB during the war. In the later stages of the war it became a Replacement Center. After returning from England in 1945 I reported to Santa Ana for processing and reassignment.

That big sprawling collection of barracks, classrooms, B.O.Q.'s, administrative buildings, mess halls, chapels, theaters, and athletic fields has disappeared from the face of the earth; it doesn't exist any more. Now located on the same land is the Orange County Fairgrounds and in September 1948 about 243 acres became the site of Orange Coast College, and another section of the land became the Costa Mesa Civic Center. Costa Mesa was not even an incorporated town until 1953. It now has over 100,000 people and the small town of Santa Ana has grown to over 300,000 population. The Costa Mesa Historical Society published a history, "The SAAAB Story" by Edrick Miller, but I could not get a copy on interlibrary loan from Santa Ana or Costa Mesa. Progress and growth has simply obliterated the Santa Ana Army Air Base. As the last line of the song says, "Joltin Joe has left and gone away; hey, hey, hey."

Eagle Field at Dos Palos was not overwhelmed by progress; it was abandoned, then forgotten. In December 1995 I returned to the location of my Primary Flight School. Driving north on Interstate 5, I noticed we were near Dos Palos so we exited the freeway and headed to town. Needing directions to find the field, I parked on the main street and asked in several stores. They never heard of Eagle Field! Finally a clerk in a liquor store gave me vague directions: west from town, then south over an irrigation canal, then west again and there were the remains of Eagle Field. Most of the buildings; the classrooms, mess hall, headquarters, control tower and the hangar were still there. Except for the headquarters building and the hangar, the other buildings had been vandalized. Above the hangar doors a sign still boldly proclaimed: EAGLE FIELD, US ARMY AIR CORPS, ELEV. 153.

It appeared as if, when the field was closed 50 years earlier, that everyone had simply walked away abandoning the airfield. Someone was using part of the old headquarters building, but I could find no one there. It was a sad and derelict place. There were parts of aircraft strewn around near the hangar and it looked as if someone was hoping to create a mini air museum. Recently I was able to verify that there is a museum at Eagle Field. Web sites identify the museum as the "Heritage of Eagles Air Museum" and also as "CCHMM" or "Central California Historical Military Museum."

Each year the museum puts on its only fund raiser, a fly-in and dinner dance/reunion held in the hangar. The last such event was on September 22, 2001. With its 2300-foot asphalt runway Eagle Field is a restricted use airport, not open to general air traffic.

The impression I got from the few people I talked to in Dos Palos was that they were unaware of the field's existence, let alone its history, the time when training planes were buzzing overhead daily, and when air cadets walked the streets of their town and had a meal in the local café, the Servatorium, long-since closed. I hope the museum can make a go of it, but Eagle Field in 1995 looked like an endangered species.

While the Santa Ana Air Base had been overwhelmed by progress and Eagle Field left to decay, the Lemoore Army Air Base had been done in by the US Navy. My assumptions had always been that the Army field, my Basic Flight School, had been taken over by the Navy after the war and had evolved into the current Lemoore Naval Air Station. To find out what had happened to the base, I talked to the historian at the Naval Air Station and on his recommendation to the helpful folks at the Carnegie Museum in Hanford, California.

The Navy historian was sympathetic but knew little about the Army field at Lemoore. His job was naval history. He did know, however, that the Lemoore Army Air Field was located south of Highway 198 and about one and a half miles west of the main gate to the Naval Air Station and that the Navy never used the old runways. They were torn up and there is no evidence of them in what is now farm fields. The Navy put in new runways north of the highway. I didn't ask if he knew that the author of the book, God Is My Copilot, Robert Scott, had been an Army pilot at Lemoore. Would he even have recognized the name?

The Carnegie Museum people told me that the first cadet class arrived at Lemoore AAF on 16 December 1941 just nine days after the Pearl Harbor attack. They also confirmed the fate of Lemoore Army Air Base; it was demolished by the US Navy. The area is now so dominated by the Naval Air Station that few people remember that there was an Army Air

Base at Lemoore. "Anchors Away, my Boys, Anchors Away" and "Sink the Army, Sink the Army Gray."

My Advanced Flight School at the Stockton Army Air Base was not destroyed after the war. It was taken over by the City of Stockton and evolved into the Stockton Metropolitan Airport. Ideally located south of the city and between the north-south corridors of Interstate Highway 5 and Highway 99, the airport supports regular passenger service and air freight. As late as 1993 some of the Army barracks and and the distinctive red and white checkerboard water tower were still standing but have now been removed. The main runways were lengthened to handle large jet aircraft. The area near the base would be hard to recognize today. From a small college town, Stockton has grown to a city of over 240,000 population. The San Joaquin Historical Society Museum and the Stockton Metropolitan Airport have maintained historical records and photos of the Stockton Army Air Base.

With the help of Audrey Hancock of the Hobbs Public Library, I learned about the fate of Hobbs Army Air Base. In 1942 it was the first four-engine transition school training pilots in the Flying Fortress. Intensive training continued into 1945. The Hobbs New-Sun reported at least ten crashes of B-17's flying from Hobbs. Deactivation started in 1946. After departure of the last soldiers in 1948, the War Assets Administration took control, selling off buildings and equipment. Hobbs officials and New Mexico senators continued to lobby for reactivation of the air base. In 1948 the City of Hobbs acquired the property. Efforts were made to develop an industrial park. Currently there are three main uses of the land: a prison, the Soaring Society of America, and a city park with a golf course. One hangar from the old base is still standing.

Dyersburg Army Air Base

If I have written anything derogatory about Dyersburg, I take it all back. This is a place with a sense of history. The people of northwestern Tennessee should be commended for what they have done to preserve the history of the Combat Crew Training Base at Dyersburg. Although the base was a drab place, with its tarpaper barracks and dusty grounds, the local people knew that the crews leaving Dyersburg could in a few short weeks be crossing the hostile skies over Germany. Knowing that truth, they also took it upon themselves to preserve the history of the base.

To build Dyersburg Army Air Base, land was condemned by the government dislocating many farm families. However, employment was provided in building the air field and on the base during the war years. A severe housing shortage was partially alleviated when towns people converted attics, garages and closets into sleeping areas for wives and loved ones visiting airmen before they went overseas.

When the air base was closed at war's end, farm land was auctioned and some buildings were moved to private property. Reportedly some equipment was driven into big holes and covered with earth. Only one of the three runways is in use; the others are in disrepair. One hangar of the original five remains along with chimneys still standing at the site of base buildings. The 95 acre concrete apron, where the B-17's were parked, is still there as witness to the many bombers flown from Dyersburg Army Air Base.

Responding to my inquiries, Tim Bivens of the Dyersburg Army Air Base Memorial Association sent copies of the orders dated 29 June 1944 transferring 56 crews (including our crew) from Dyersburg to the Army Air Field at Kearney, Nebraska. The army field has been renamed Arnold Field. Located on the site of the base is the Veterans Museum. Like the museum's brochure states, all that remains of the Army Air Base is hundreds of acres of concrete. The Dyersburg AAB Memorial Association in conjunction with the museum put on a yearly fly-in and warbird air show the last weekend of August to memorialize the Dyersburg Army Air Base.

Although the Army Air Base at Dyersburg was operational for only three years (1942 to 1945) it had a major impact on the nearby communities. Perhaps the south is more aware than other parts of the country of the influence of history. I salute the efforts of the people of the DAAB Memorial Association and of the Veterans Museum in preserving the history of their air base. One day I hope to return to Dyersburg.

Kearney Army Air Base

Kearney, Nebraska, was a special place for air crews. We knew that our stay at Kearney AAF would be short; we were there only seven days, 1 July to 7 July 1944. But subconsciously air crews knew that this town could be their last glimpse of the USA and what was to them home. I think that the townspeople recognized this feeling and because they did, a special relationship existed between the Kearney people and the airmen.

With the gracious help of Cindy Messinger, Reference Librarian at the Kearney Public Library, I learned much about the history of Kearney Army Air Base, both during and after the war. She sent me information on the air base from the publication, Kearney 125 (1873-1998), a Quasquicentennial History" edited by P. S. Holmgren , Ph.D. and from a masters thesis on the "History of Kearney Army Air Field" by Todd L. Peterson.

I learned that five days after 24 August 1942 when Kearney dedicated its new F.G. Keens Municipal Airport, the Army announced they wanted the airport. The city signed a lease for as long as the airport was needed. The Army condemned over 2200 additional acres of farmland for the air base. Thousands of construction workers were employed and by January 1943 the base was functional. The first B-17 squadron arrived in February, part of the 100th Bomb Group, later to become famous with the 8th Air Force as the "Bloody 100th." Kearney AAF was a Combat Crew Training Center from August to November 1943 when the Training Group was transferred to Sioux City, Iowa. The base then became a processing center for B-17 crews and later for B-29 crews where these crews picked up new planes to fly overseas.

The City of Kearney was important to the base and its citizens provided all kinds of services for the airmen. They raised money and built a recreational facility which became a USO Center, a home away from home for servicemen. Aware that the segregated black troops would need a facility, a local committee rented a building and converted it into a recreational center.

After WWII a fighter wing, the 27th, was stationed at Kearney. It was moved in February 1949 and in March the Kearney Air Force Base was declared excess. Subsequently the air base was returned to the town and today it is the Kearney Municipal Airport. The buildings on the base were not destroyed. Many were moved into Kearney, the base chapel becoming a Lutheran Church. Some of the two story housing units are still used as apartment complexes in Kearney. Dozens of the other smaller base buildings were moved to the city for other uses.

The people of Kearney did not forget their Army Air Base. In 1988 a joint committee of the Historical Society and the Chamber of Commerce staged a three-day reunion for people who had served at the base. During the war years, hospitality was the rule, not the exception in Kearney. They have memorialized the Army Air Base and the air crews that passed through Kearney in the best way—by productive use of the field and its buildings.

As the University of Nebraska song says: "There Is No Place Like Nebraska."

USAAF Station 167, Ridgewell, England

There is something about the place that speaks to us, we former members of the 381st Bomb Group. We can still hear the sound of radial engines, feel the East Anglia wind and see the vast low gray cloud cover. More than that, when here, we can again feel the kinship with people in this foreign land. It is because the people of Ridgewell and surrounding villages understood the air war and what we were risking on each mission. They sweated out the return of our planes, took us into their homes, and would share a pint at the local pub. Through the years the mutual respect between the US airmen and the villagers has endured.

The air field at Ridgewell is mostly gone, the runways removed and the land returned to farming. My first return to Ridgewell was in 1983. On that occasion we drove through the villages of Clare, Ovington, Ashen, and Great Yeldham, all near our Ridgewell air base. We visited the site of the 381st Bomb Group Memorial. It had been dedicated on 28 August 1982 at a ceremony attended by many 381st veterans and an overflow crowd of local people. Ellis Richard and Gene Nelson represented our crew at the dedication. Both of our chaplains, Dr. James Good Brown and Father Andrew Strednak, were present. Rev. John Duncan of Ridgewell gave the invocation. The national anthems of both countries, the USA and Great Britain, were played by the Haverhill Brass Band and the colors were presented by a USAF Color Guard from Mildenhall AFB.

Pearl Garrod, who lives in a nearby bungalow, gave the memorial land in perpetuity to the 381st BG(H) Memorial Association. Her brother farms the land and I am told that Pearl washes "calling cards" left by birds from the memorial stone. There is now a 381st BG Museum a few yards from the memorial located in one of the remaining Nissen huts. It stems from a collection of Tony Ince, from Ashen, who collected items over the years, many dug up from nearby land. A few other Nissen huts are still used as farm buildings.

So we of the 381at Bomb Group have a memorial near our air base in England, a land of history and memorials. The monument near Ridgewell is registered with the American Battle Monuments Commission as an official Battle Monument of the USA. But the memories and our history are preserved by people, as well as in granite, and we of the 381st have some exceptional British friends doing just that. On Memorial Day our friends never fail to lay a wreath at the American Military Cemetery at Maddingly, England. Dave Osborne, Ron Mackay and Derek Cross are a few of our many close friends in England, writing history and always available to greet a 381st visitor.

And in turn, the members of the 381st Memorial Association have responded to The kindness of friends near Ridgewell. Funds have been contributed to help with needed restoration of the 11th Century church in Ashen and to help pay for a stained glass window in the Congregational Church at Ridgewell.

Maybe not hallowed ground, but we of the 381st consider Ridgewell as our small part of "this scepter'd isle."

POSTSCRIPT

This narrative has covered only a fraction of our crew's stories and those were mainly based on my recollection of events. There are many untold stories written in the skies over Europe that, if not forgotten, are now dim in our memories. The details of some experiences may be obscure, but the feelings and impressions of our time as an air crew remain with us today.

What about our state of mind? Very new to the experience of flight, did we have misgivings about being part of an air crew? Any doubts we had about joining the Army Air Force were probably outweighed by the glamour associated with flying. In the 1940's the vast majority of people had never been in an airplane. The media of the time portrayed the airman as a dashing personality, unique in the military service. That image and the challenge of flight may have influenced our choice.

During our training as gunners, radio operators, flight engineers, bombardiers, navigators or pilots our concern was to succeed and not become "washouts." The danger of training accidents, some fatal, was pushed to the back of our minds. The unique camaraderie developed in combat crew training school and during our flight to the British Isles made us each more confident.

Then one morning in August of 1944 we faced our first combat mission. Amazingly, despite all of the overwhelming evidence to the contrary, when we climbed on board our B-17 that morning we didn't really think anything bad was going to happen to us. We were too green to know better. Our concern was to do everything right. It didn't take many missions to learn about fear. Each of us would handle the emotion differently. But I am sure that at one time or another we were all scared to death by what we saw in the sky over Germany. We saw nearby planes in our formation go down in flames. We saw the flak barrage ahead and felt defenseless on the bomb run, knowing we were going to fly straight and level into the black bursts. We could not let our fear affect our responsibility to the crew.

In recent years some people have raised the moral question of the bombing of enemy cities with the resulting civilian casualties. At the time I do not recall anyone doubting the rightness of our efforts. Our generation knew that Nazi Germany had to be stopped. Of course we knew about the indiscriminate bombing by German planes of cities in Poland, Holland, and England. Although it was apparent that our bombs often went astray we were always briefed for specific industrial or military targets. We believed in what we were doing and that our efforts would shorten the war.

We were together as an air crew for less than a year. Although the time was short, the learning curve was sharp and intense. We learned what commitment to a team effort could accomplish. We learned how to work together with others from diverse ethnic, religious and geographic backgrounds. Tested by the strife and adversity of the war, our understanding of people and the world we live in was enhanced.

We wouldn't want to do it again, but we wouldn't have missed our time together for anything. Looking back, I think we are all astonished by who we were and what we did. Had I not known each member of our crew I would be a different person today, diminished in some way. Maybe that's the sum-up: the value added to a life by knowing such people, devoted to a cause and to each other.

Addendum:

And now we are four. In 2003, Hugh Treadwell, with his family, made a pilgrimage to our old air base at Ridgewell. That October, Hugh and Edith hosted a crew reunion in El Paso, Texas. They gave each of us a fragment from the Ridgewell control tower, mounted on a plaque. In January of 2005 Hugh passed away, his Final Approach. We miss him.

Since the last printing of this book in April 2007 we have lost another crew member, our intrepid copilot, Ellis Richard. Rich died in June 2007. His name is to be inscribed on The Star of Honor Fountain at the Veterans Cemetery in Sonoma, CA.

Another of our aircrew has gone to the *Wild Blue Yonder*. Rudy Staszko, our super Flight Engineer, Top Turret Gunner and Senior Sergeant, having survived through Veterans Day in 2009, died in the early hours of November 12. We salute you, Rudy.

On June 28, 2012 I ordered flowers for the funeral in Cedarburg, Wisconsin of Eugene L. Nelson. Gene died on Monday, June 25, 2012. Now I am the last of our crew, flying solo again. With the flowers I wrote:

> *"In honor of our Navigator, our comrade and our friend Eugene L. Nelson. He showed us the way! On behalf of the entire aircrew, we salute you, Gene."*
>
> Ed and Jan Carr

Selected Bibliography

BOOKS OF THE EIGHTH AIR FORCE AND THE B-17

Appleby, John. *Suffolk Summer.* Ipswich: East Anglia Magazine, 1948.

Astor, Gerald. *The Mighty Eighth.* New York: Dell Publishing, 1997.

Bendiner, Elmer. *The Fall of Fortresses.* New York: Putnam, 1980.

Caidin, Martin. *Flying Forts, The B-17 in World War II.* New York: Ballantine Books, 1969; Bantam Edition, 1990.

Chant, Chris. *Air Forces of World War I and World War II.* London: Quarto Publishing, 1979.

Crosby, Harry. *A Wing and a Prayer.* New York: Harper Collins, 1993.

Fletcher, Eugene. *The Lucky Bastard Club Fletcher's Gang.* Seattle: UW Press, 1988.

Freeman, Roger. *B-17 Fortresses at War—The Mighty Eighth, a History.* London: McDonald & Co., 1970.

Freeman, Roger and Osborne, David. *The B-17 Flying Fortress Story.* London: Arms & Armour Press, 1998.

Halpert, Sam. *A Real Good War.* St. Petersburg, Florida: Southern Heritage Press, 1997.

Hawkins, Ian. *B-17's Over Berlin.* Washington: Brassey's (US), 1990.

Jablonski, Edward. *Flying Fortress.* New York: Doubleday & Co., 1965.

_____, *America in the Air.* Chicago: Time-Life Books, 1982.

Kaplan, Philip and Smith, Rex. *One Last Look.* New York: Abbeville Press, 1983.

Klinkowitz, Jerome. *Yanks over Europe.* Lexington, KY: University Press of Kentucky, 1996.

Lay, Bernie and Bartlett, Sy. *Twelve O'Clock High.* New York: Harper & Brothers, 1948.

McCarthy, David. *Fear No More.* Pittsburgh: Cottage Wordsmiths, 1991.

McManus, John. *Deadly Sky.* Navato, CA: Presidio Press, 2000.

O'Neill, Brian. *Half a Wing, Three Engines and a Prayer.* Blue Ridge Summit, PA: Tab BooksInc., 1989.

Perret, Geoffrey. *Winged Victory.* New York: Random House, 1993.

Rogers, Eugene. *Flying High.* New York: Atlantic Monthly Press, 1996

Woolnough, John. *Stories of the Eighth.* Hollywood, FL: The 8th AF News, 1983

Continued

BOOKS OF THE 381st BOMB GROUP

Brown, James Good (Chaplain). *Mighty Men of the 381st, Heroes All.* Salt Lake City: Publishers Press, 1984.
Mackay, Ron. *381st Bomb Group.* Carrollton, TX: Squadron/Signal Publ. Inc. 1994.
Osborne, David. *They Came From Over the Pond.* Madison, WI: 381st Memorial Assoc., 1999.
Stone, Ken. *Triumphant We Fly.* Paducah, KY: Turner Publishing, 1994.

MOVIES OF THE EIGHTH AIR FORCE

Command Decision
Memphis Belle (A documentary and a movie)
Twelve O'Clock High
The War Lover

TELEVISION PROGRAMS OF THE EIGHTH AIR FORCE

All the Brave Young Men (NBC Documentary)
Twelve O'Clock High (TV Drama Series)
We'll Meet Again (British TV Drama Series)

Index

The Aftermath – Crew Reunions

Omaha 1978
L – R Standing: Rudy Staszko, Gene Nelson, Ed Carr
Kneeling: Rob Whitaker, Ellis Richard

Seattle 1985
L – R: Ed Carr, Gene Nelson, Jan Carr, Rudy Staszko

Seattle 1985

L – R: Gene Nelson, Al Hines, Rudy Staszko, Ed Carr, Ellis Richard, Rob Whitaker

(Hugh Treadwell attended, but not in photo)

San Francisco 1995
L – R: Hugh Treadwell, Ed Carr. Ellis Richard, Gene Nelson

Neshkoro, Wisconsin 2000
L – R: Ellis Richard, Ed Carr, Gene Nelson

Whidbey Island, WA 2001
L – R: Ed Carr, Edith Treadwell, Hugh Treadwell, Gene Nelson, Pat Pagliaro,
Robin Richard, Ellis Richard

Sonoma, CA 2002
L – R: Gene Nelson, Pat Pagliaro, Edith Treadwell, Jan Carr, Ed Carr, Robin Richard,
Hugh Treadwell, Ellis Richard